INSTITUTE OF LEADERSHIP & MANAGEMENT **ilm**

SUPERSERIES

Planning Training and Development

FOURTH EDITION

Published for the
Institute of Leadership & Management by **Pergamon Flexible Learning**

OXFORD   AMSTERDAM   BOSTON   LONDON   NEW YORK   PARIS
SAN DIEGO   SAN FRANCISCO   SINGAPORE   SYDNEY   TOKYO

Pergamon Flexible Learning
An imprint of Elsevier Science
Linacre House, Jordan Hill, Oxford OX2 8DP
200 Wheeler Road, Burlington, MA 01803

First published 1986
Second edition 1991
Third edition 1997
Fourth edition 2003

British Library Cataloguing in Publication Data
A catalogue record for this book is available from the British Library

ISBN 0 7506 5860 6

For information on Pergamon Flexible Learning
visit our website at www.bh.com/pergamonfl

Institute of Leadership & Management
registered office
1 Giltspur Street
London
EC1A 9DD
Telephone 020 7294 3053
www.i-l-m.com
ILM is a subsidiary of the City & Guilds Group

The views expressed in this work are those of the authors and do
not necessarily reflect those of the Institute of Leadership &
Management or of the publisher

Authors: Alison Allenby and Dela Jenkins
Editor: Dela Jenkins
Editorial management: Genesys, www.genesys-consultants.com
Based on previous material by: Joe Johnson
Composition by Genesis Typesetting, Rochester, Kent
Printed and bound in Great Britain by MPG Books, Bodmin

Contents

Contents

Workbook introduction

1 ILM Super Series study links

This workbook addresses the issues of *Planning Training and Development*. Should you wish to extend your study to other Super Series workbooks covering related or different subject areas, you will find a comprehensive list at the back of this book.

In particular, you are advised to look at the companion workbook to this one, *Delivering Training*, which, together with this workbook, will give you a complete understanding of the four-stage cycle which underpins the whole subject of training preparation and delivery.

2 Links to ILM Qualifications

This workbook relates to the following learning outcomes in segments from the ILM Level 3 Introductory Certificate in First Line Management and the Level 3 Certificate in First Line Management.

C7.3 Planning Development
1 Identify development needs in conjunction with the staff concerned
2 Understand a range of approaches and techniques and their application in the workplace
3 Agree development plan(s) with staff to meet their identified needs, taking account of resource implications

3 Links to S/NVQs in Management

This workbook relates to the following elements of the Management Standards which are used in S/NVQs in Management, as well as a range of other S/NVQs.

C9.1   Contribute to the identification of development needs
C9.3   Contribute to development activities

It will also help you to develop the following Personal Competences:

■   communicating;
■   thinking and taking decisions.

4 Workbook objectives

As a manager you will almost certainly have some responsibility for coaching and training your workteam. You will be expected to carry out or organize different types of development activities. This will include induction training when new employees start work and need introducing to the environment in which they are to work, their work colleagues and the job that they are expected to do. You may also be expected to carry out ongoing job training, which may include refresher training, introducing new tasks to individuals or introducing totally new skills to the workteam. Occasionally you may also be called upon to carry out specific training, such as safety training.

Skills development is a complicated process. The simplest way to approach it is to divide it into four stages:

Stage 1 – Assessing training needs
Stage 2 – Planning and preparation
Stage 3 – Delivering the training
Stage 4 – Giving feedback, evaluating the results and providing further support as necessary.

This workbook concentrates on the first and second stages, assessing training needs, and planning and preparation. The next two stages are discussed in another workbook in this series, *Delivering Training*, which also looks at the ways in which you can support your team members through coaching, counselling and mentoring.

Imagine that in your workteam you have recently gained two new employees. One has some experience of the type of work you do but the other is totally new to it. How would you go about developing them? What tasks and skills would they need to improve? Who would train them, when and how long would it take? These are all questions that you would need to answer. You would also need to look at each individual and decide what each needed to learn in order to carry out the job he or she had been employed to do.

To carry out this role effectively you would need to develop certain skills yourself. This workbook will introduce you to and help you develop these essential skills.

Session A discusses what is meant by training, and its benefits to you, the organization and the trainees. It also introduces the concept of the training cycle.

When planning training you need to be able to identify training needs that would help both individuals and workteams meet work objectives. This requires you to collect and analyse information and present it to others for discussion or approval. Training needs analysis is discussed in Session B.

In Session C you will learn how to plan training in an organized and scheduled manner and take into account all the resources that are available. Planning training happens in a variety of ways in different workplaces. In some organizations this is done in a very formal and structured way and in others it is more simple. However it is done, it is important that it is done well – the future of your workteam and your workplace may depend upon it.

This workbook will help produce training plans that will be effective.

4.1 Objectives

When you have completed this workbook you will be better able to:

- describe the importance and benefits of training to you, your workteam and the organization you work for;
- use different techniques to collect and analyse information for training needs analysis purposes;
- contribute to the identification of training and development needs for individuals and workteams;
- set objectives for training and development;
- contribute to planning training and development;
- draw up a training plan.

5 Activity planner

The following Activities require some planning so you may want to look at these now.

- Activity 21 on page 39 asks you to analyse the skills needed to carry out a particular job.
- Activity 23 on page 44 looks at versatility charts
- Activity 26 on page 49 asks you to look at your organization's performance appraisal system
- Activity 30 on page 59 is concerned with initial assessment plans
- Activity 36 on page 74 asks you to complete an induction training planning form
- Activity 38 on page 77 asks you to record a training plan.

Some or all of these Activities may provide the basis of evidence for your S/NVQ portfolio. Activities and the work-based assignment are signposted with this icon.

The icon states the elements to which the Portfolio Activities and Work-based assignment relate.

The work-based assignment on page 85 is designed to help you meet Elements C9.1 (Contribute to the identification of development needs) and C9.3 (Contribute to development activities) of the Management Standards. You may want to prepare for it in advance.

Session A
The importance of training

1 Introduction

Many organizations invest a lot of time and money in developing their people. The methods used vary between organizations but will include things like training courses and coaching. Obviously organizations expect their investment to pay dividends in terms of increased productivity and profitability. So what can an organization do to ensure that it gets the results it wants from its training? This workbook sets out the steps that should be taken to ensure that the right training is given to the right people at the right time.

In order to do this it is essential that we first clarify exactly what we mean by training. Although it seems to be a simple enough concept, many aspects of training do appear to be frequently misunderstood. Some people have trouble in defining exactly what training is and is not. The benefits of training, both to the organization and to the individual, are sometimes underestimated.

Training is not just sending someone away on a course. Although sometimes external training courses are exactly what individuals need to improve their skills, there are many other effective development methods that can be used. Coaching or mentoring time given by an experienced person to a less experienced person can bring about impressive results and has the added benefit of being delivered internally.

We will start to explain some of these processes to you by introducing you to the training cycle. This will then prepare the ground for the rest of this workbook.

2 What do we mean by training?

'Training' is a commonly used word that may be applied to a variety of activities. As a manager you will probably have received some kind of training and may have given training to others.

Activity 1 · 3 mins

Tick all those Activities listed below that you would consider to be training.

a   A workteam leader showing a workteam member how to operate a machine. ☐

b   A new shop assistant learning how to operate a till by observing how a more experienced assistant does it. ☐

c   An instructor lecturing to a group of nurses on the application of a new medical procedure. ☐

d   A demonstration of the operation of fire-fighting equipment to a group of firefighters. ☐

e   A workteam member attending a local training centre on a day-release scheme. ☐

f   A technician spending a week on a residential course on quality control procedures. ☐

g   A manager briefing his/her workteam. ☐

h   A personnel expert giving guidance to a manager on appraisal interviews. ☐

i   A manager watching a receptionist dealing with a difficult caller. ☐

j   Police recruits practising firearm skills. ☐

k   A new sales person accompanying another experienced person on some sales visits. ☐

l   Attending an evening class for 'Holiday Spanish Conversation'. ☐

m   Attending a pre-natal child care course. ☐

n   A group of students attending a graduate course in English literature. ☐

It would not be unreasonable to tick all these Activities. The list illustrates the variety of forms that training can take.

However, we can ignore the last three items on the list as they are not relevant to work (on the whole). Training concentrates on building up knowledge, skills and attitudes which are directly relevant to work.

As for item (n) – students taking a course in English literature – you may have decided, quite rightly, that this comes under the heading of 'education' rather than training. Without going into all the meanings of these two words we can generally reckon education to be less vocationally specific and tending to deal with hypotheses rather than specific instances.

In this workbook we will only be concerned with work-related training that contains specific objectives.

Activity 2
3 mins

When you attend training courses or sessions at work, what, in general terms do you hope to gain from them? Give your answer briefly in the space below.

_____

_____

_____

_____

You may have said things like:

- 'knowledge', 'expertise', 'skills', 'knowhow' or 'information';
- the means of doing your job better;
- the means of increasing your earning power;
- the means of developing your potential.

Improving effectiveness at work.

All these would be good answers to the question, and in a sense they all come to the same thing. We could say that, in broad terms

training is designed to improve the effectiveness of people at work, because training provides a means of acquiring skills and knowledge.

4

By acquiring skills and knowledge people are better able to:

- carry out their jobs;
- earn more money;
- develop as individuals.

Of course there are lots of ways of acquiring skills and knowledge, but does it matter **how** it is done? Read the example below and answer the questions in the Activity that follows.

Connie, a school leaver, started a new job as an administrative assistant in an office. There were two other people in the office, Jackie and Warren. At the interview for the job, Connie was told that she'd be expected to 'be generally useful – take messages, that kind of thing'.

On the first day it became obvious to Connie that the office was a very busy one. People were coming in and out all the time, leaving instructions, asking for information and so on. And the 'phone never stopped ringing'. Connie was 'in at the deep end' from the start. Neither Jackie nor Warren had much time to tell her what to do. They told her 'Not to worry – just watch and learn – and if someone gives you a message, write it down.' From time to time, when Connie asked for help, either Jackie or Warren would try to find five minutes to tell her about a particular form or procedure. Although Connie wasn't used to any of this, she was a bright girl and after a while she started to become a useful member of the workteam.

Connie acquired knowledge and improved her skills through observation and from the snippets of information she picked up as she went along. Later on, another new person started work in the office and Connie was introduced as being **'fully trained and experienced in the job'**.

Activity 3

5 mins

a So Connie learned how to do the job – but was she trained?   Yes/No

b Do you think that most school leavers, being put in the situation Connie was in, would have succeeded in becoming proficient?   Yes/No

c If you were a manager in that office, say briefly what you would have done differently in introducing Connie to the job.

_____

_____

_____

_____

_____

It seems obvious that Connie was **not** trained. Few school leavers would have managed to overcome the difficulties she had to face. Connie learned how to do her job **in spite of** the lack of training. 'Training' is too grand a word to use for the casual conversations she had with her colleagues.

To be worthy of the name, and to be effective, training must be **planned** and **organized**.

Training is a planned and organized procedure.

As was the case with Connie, people sometimes learn to do their jobs in spite of lack of training. However, it would be foolish to expect this kind of haphazard method to succeed in most situations. So we can say that:

Training is a planned and organized procedure designed to improve the effectiveness of people at work.

By 'planned' we mean that the training is specifically designed to meet defined needs. So it is essential that managers be involved in the process and develop the necessary skills to carry out the task competently.

3 Effective training

Even when training is planned and organized, there are some occasions when it is not as effective as it might be. Consider these three cases:

Jeremy Chesterfield was listening to a talk about safety at work. The lecturer was describing some terrible accidents that had occurred at other companies similar to his. He was emphasizing the need for being strict about obeying safety rules and not 'cutting corners'.

Jeremy wasn't convinced. He thought that these accidents had probably been caused by sheer carelessness or stupidity. Jeremy felt that if he followed every safety instruction to the letter he would never get his job done. He let the talk 'go in one ear and out the other'.

Shula Evans sat glumly in front of the computer screen. Along with her fellow supervisors she was taking part in an introductory training session about the hospital's new method of keeping patients' records. For years Shula had been keeping these records on file cards. She was efficient, the system worked and she couldn't see the need to 'computerize' everything. Apart from everything else, Shula was not confident that she would cope with the new system.

Vicky Sikopoulis was having great difficulties. She worked for a firm of training specialists and she had been called into the Fairweather Optical Company to give a training session to the company's managers on 'Continuous Improvement Groups'. The problem was that most of her audience did not seem convinced about the concept. There was a lot of criticism of the whole idea and she was constantly being interrupted.

Activity 4

10 mins

In each of the three cases the training wasn't as successful as it might have been. What was the problem in each case?

Jeremy Chesterfield's problem was:

_____

_____

Shula Evans's problem was:

_____

_____

Vicky Sikopoulis's audience's problem was:

_____

_____

The common problem that prevented all these three training sessions being more successful was the attitude of the trainees. They were not in a receptive frame of mind.

> In Jeremy's case he didn't believe what the lecturer was saying and consequently didn't take in the information he was being given.
>
> In Shula's case she didn't understand the need for computerization and was afraid that she would not be able to cope with the new system. This made her defensive and not open to new ideas.
>
> Vicky's audience would have to be convinced of the value of Continuous Improvement Groups before they were willing to listen to her description of their operation.

The key is **wanting** to learn.

Human beings aren't receptive to new ideas if they can't see their value or relevance. Therefore before managers start to plan any training they will have to create an environment in which people want to be trained.

The key to learning is **wanting** to learn. People who want to learn will learn. People who don't, won't.

8

Ranjit had been called into the office of David Brierley, his manager.

'Good news, Ranjit!' David said. 'That contract we were hoping for has finally come through. Obviously your workteam will be involved. From next Monday I want you to hand over your current work to Sarah Page's group. The Hersey contract is now your top priority.'

Ranjit was very pleased with this news because he knew what it would mean to his workteam. It was clearly time that some of them got a better opportunity to use their skills and experience. They had all been hoping to have the chance to work on the Hersey contract because it was 'state of the art' technology.

David continued, 'Of course there will be a great deal to learn. Every one of you will need to attend training courses on the new equipment and because of the timescales, you'll have to be fully acquainted with lots of new concepts in a very short time. If this thing is to go well it will need a great deal of commitment on the part of everyone involved.'

Ranjit replied, 'You need have no worries on that score.'

When an organization obtains a big new contract it isn't only the directors and shareholders who are pleased. It can mean a good deal to the employees too.

Activity 5 · 5 mins

Put yourself in the position of one of Ranjit's workteam. You are a skilled and experienced worker but have been working on the same kind of equipment for some time now and you are feeling a little bored and frustrated.

Then your manager announces that you will get the opportunity to learn about the latest technology, provided you give a high level of commitment to the training and the work.

1 Is it likely that you will give your heartfelt commitment? Yes/No

2 If you do give this commitment, is your main motivation
for doing so likely to be:

- a desire to see the organization do well? ☐

- a desire for your own individual development? ☐

- a combination of these? ☐

Almost everyone in this position would be willing to give a genuine commitment to the training and the work. And in most cases, the motivation would be both a desire for personal development and a desire to promote the organization's interests.

This illustrates a strong argument in favour of training.

- A motivated workforce is more likely to achieve organizational objectives.

- Self-development is a great motivator.

- Training plays an important part in helping individuals develop.

- So training is likely to be good for the whole organization.

Training opens doors. The forward looking organization plans for the future. It will aim to meet its requirements for team leaders, managers and specialist staff from among its existing employees. By providing the training and resources for individuals to develop, an employer is not only providing an incentive for the staff – it is making an investment for the future.

4 The benefits of training

Any case for training will have to be supported by convincing arguments about the benefits that will result. These have to include business benefits to the organization as well as personal development benefits to the individual.

4.1 Benefits to the organization

Activity 6   5 mins

From your own experience and from what we've discussed so far in this session, what benefits can you think of that training brings to the organization? Try to note **two** benefits.

_____

_____

_____

_____

_____

From the organization's viewpoint, training:

- reduces learning time, so bringing new recruits to full working capacity more quickly;
- provides a means of getting jobs done more efficiently, effectively and safely;
- results in a workforce which is more flexible and better able to cope with change;
- improves the morale and motivation of employees, so making them more willing to further the objectives of the organization;
- reduces the number of customer complaints and improves relationships with customers;
- reduces the number of problems with suppliers as goods will be better specified and defects spotted more quickly;
- makes the organization more profitable through increased output or reduced costs.

Let's look at these important points in more detail.

- Training reduces learning time.

Reduced learning time.

When a new employee starts work, or when there's a new job to be learned by an existing workteam member, time can be vitally important. Modern businesses have to be extremely competitive and that often means that they cannot afford individuals to be less than fully effective for very long.

We've all seen the difference in performance between a trained worker and one who is untrained.

■ Training provides a means of getting jobs done more efficiently, effectively and safely.

Activity 7 · 5 mins

Think of your own workteam or section and write down an example of where training one or all of them resulted in improved performance. State exactly what positive results the training had.

_____

_____

_____

_____

_____

Your example will obviously be individual but it will probably have included results like:

- working more quickly;
- reduced waste of material and energy;
- ability to produce new product or service;
- improved delivery times;
- improved quality of service;
- reduction in the accident level.

■ Training results in a workforce that is more flexible and better able to cope with change. It also improves morale and motivation, making employees more willing to further the organization's objectives.

■ A significant part of any workteam leader's job is concerned with getting the workteam to implement management objectives. If morale is low and the workteam have little motivation that job becomes very difficult. Training often helps to improve morale and motivation because:

it can trigger a new interest in the job and open up new possibilities for the individual	it increases job security because work output can be increased and more skilful tasks can be performed

■ Training reduces the number of customer complaints. The relationship with customers is improved because the quality of products is higher, and the employees are more skilled in customer care.

■ Training reduces the number of problems with suppliers because the employees will be able to provide better specifications for goods ordered and spot defects more quickly.

■ Training makes organizations more profitable through increased output or reduced costs.

This is the bottom line for any organization. Any investment it makes in training needs to result in an economic gain.

While discussing the benefits of training to an organization it hasn't been easy to separate those benefits between employers and employees. This is because the benefits aren't all one way – individuals benefit too.

4.2 Benefits to the individual

Sometimes individuals see training as just more work, so you need to be prepared to convince them of the personal benefits. What are they likely to be?

Activity 8

We've already discussed several of the benefits of training to individual employees. For the record jot down **three** of these.

_____

_____

_____

_____

_____

You might have mentioned:

■ Increased job satisfaction

Being trained to do a job well generally makes that job much more interesting and satisfying.

- Improved self-esteem

Trained individuals take more pride in their professionalism.

- A greater potential for promotion

Increased skills and knowledge make employees more valuable to the organization. Training often gives employees the opportunity to show the organization what they are capable of doing and what their potential is. This encourages organizations to look internally when filling vacancies.

- Increased opportunities

One skill can act as a basis for learning another. (For instance, someone who has trained to carry out stock taking will be better positioned to become a stock controller in the future.)

This brings us back to the theme of personal development. People at work generally need to feel that they are making progress in some way. Not everyone wants promotion and the responsibility which comes with it. But for most people, it is demoralizing having to do the same job in the same way for a long time.

4.3 Benefits to the manager

Managers obviously benefit from having a well-trained workteam. Many of the benefits we have already listed will also be beneficial to the manager, such as:

- getting work done more safely, efficiently and effectively;
- improved workteam morale;
- greater flexibility, enabling change to be managed more easily.

But there are more specific advantages for someone like you. For example, how much of your time do you spend 'fire fighting' – dealing with urgent problems which your workteam members can't cope with? With better training they might be able to handle things better on their own, rather than having to call on you every time something unexpected happens.

You will probably be happier about delegating responsibility too, if you know that the people standing in for you have been well trained.

And of course, a trained workteam is a much more flexible one: people are able to cover for absent colleagues more easily and deal more effectively with unexpected situations.

5 Alternatives to training

Consideration of whether to go ahead with training should include an appraisal of the alternatives and the cost and benefits associated with them.

Activity 9

2 mins

So far we've discussed all the positive aspects of training. But it's often hard to sell the benefits of training. Make a note of **at least two** objections you have heard (or perhaps have made yourself) when training has been suggested.

_____

_____

_____

_____

_____

You might have mentioned the costs of providing training, which can be very considerable.

Apart from the costs of the training itself – the trainer, the equipment, the accommodation and so on – there is the fact that, while being trained, employees are not working. This sort of lost time is a real concern to any manager. Fortunately on-the-job training and mentoring can greatly reduce the amount of time that a person needs to spend away from work. You can learn more about mentoring in _Delivering Training_ in this series.

You could also have noted the fact that trained personnel are likely to find it easier to change jobs. Many an employer has invested a great deal in the training of key workers, only to find them leave the organization shortly afterwards for a better paid job elsewhere.

There are other disadvantages. One is the problem of who does the training. If it is done 'on the job' the people who are best at doing the work may not be the best at imparting their knowledge. Also such skilled and knowledgeable workers are often needed on other tasks.

If training is carried out 'off the job' using dedicated trainers, there is a difficulty in making sure that the trainers understand the way your organization operates.

Activity 10

2 mins

Are there any alternatives to training? Can you think of **at least one** alternative?

_____

_____

_____

_____

Assuming that trained workers are needed, one option for an employer is to only recruit new employees who have already reached the required standards. This is really taking advantage of the training given by others and you will probably have to offer higher wages.

Another alternative is work simplification. At one extreme this can consist of breaking a large job into two or three smaller sections so that it can be tackled by a workteam, rather than by an individual. At the other extreme it can mean completely de-skilling a job so that virtually no training is needed to do the work. The disadvantages, however, are considerable and include low employee morale and a high incidence of industrial disputes.

One other alternative is to use subcontracted labour who already have the required expertise. This may be very helpful in the short term but you will have to pay these people at a higher rate.

So in spite of the apparent costs of training, the alternatives are seldom cheaper in the long run. And as we've already seen, the benefits of training are many and varied.

6 The training cycle

We've already discussed the fact that training needs to be carried out in a systematic way to be successful. Now let's be more specific about this.

There are four systematic stages which comprise **the training cycle** but before we look at these let's start by looking at the case of 'Gwyneth and the undertrained clerks'.

When Gwyneth Roberts took over as manager of the general office, she wasn't very impressed with what she found. For one thing, the 'training programme' really existed in name only. On investigation, Gwyneth found that:

- when new starters joined, after spending a couple of days with the previous manager, they were for the most part simply left to learn what they could by sitting next to one of the more experienced clerks;
- there was no proper record of who was trained to carry out what task, so it was difficult to say what the office's training needs were;
- no-one monitored the progress of clerks as they picked up the job;
- no-one had much idea of how successful the training was;
- when certain members of staff went sick or took a day off, it was very difficult to find anyone else in the office who could stand in for them.

Gwyneth obviously had a big job in front of her to organize the training.

Activity 11

3 mins

Imagine that Gwyneth asked for your advice about where to start with the organizing of her training. What would you suggest she did first?

_____

_____

_____

_____

Your response may have been to say that the first thing to be done is to identify just what training is required. This is correct because until Gwyneth knows who needs what training, she can't begin to get anything organized.

To do this systematically Gwyneth will need to be clear in her mind about what her workteam's overall **objectives** are. She will need to ask herself the question:

> 'What does the organization want my workteam to achieve?'

The objectives of the workteam must, of course, be compatible with the objectives of the whole organization. If Gwyneth isn't clear about what her workteam's objectives are then she will need to talk to her boss and clarify exactly what they are. These objectives will then give her targets or goals against which she can measure how well her workteam are doing. It will enable her to ask questions like:

'How well is the workteam performing compared with the way I'd like it to perform?'

'What more do workteam members need to know and understand?'

'What skills do individual workteam members have, compared with the skills they need to do the job well?'

'Is the workteam actually doing what it should really be doing?'

If the way that things are at present is not the same as the way we'd like them to be, then there is obviously a **performance gap**. Here is a diagram to show these points.

Now the way to improve the skills and knowledge of the workteam is through training. Therefore the performance gap is also the extent of the **training need**.

So now we're in a position to spell out the first stage in the training cycle.

6.1 Training cycle stage 1 – Identify the training needs

```
                    1
               Identify the
              training needs
```

In this first stage Gwyneth must:

■ define the objectives of the workteam within the overall objectives of the organization;
■ identify the performance gap or training need between what **is** being achieved and what **should be** achieved;
■ pinpoint the differences between the **actual** skill levels and the skill levels **needed** for the job.

The whole subject of identifying training needs is discussed in depth in Session B.

Gwyneth's next step is to consider what sort of training programme will meet the training needs.

6.2 Training cycle stage 2 – Making plans and preparations

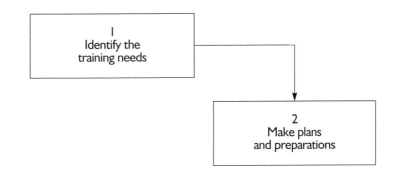

In order to make plans and prepare for training Gwyneth must be able to:

- define the training objectives;
- identify the course content;
- decide in what order and to what depth it should be learned;
- decide what methods of training are to be used;
- identify who is to learn what;
- plan where and when the training is to take place;
- identify what resources might be needed;
- estimate costs;
- decide who is to support the trainees at work when they come to try out their new skills;
- plan how she will manage to keep the office running while the training is taking place;
- decide who will be involved in giving the training;
- decide how the results will be assessed.

We will consider the answers to these questions in Session C.

Once the plan is in place and the preparations are complete, the training programme can begin.

6.3 Training cycle stage 3 – Implement the plans

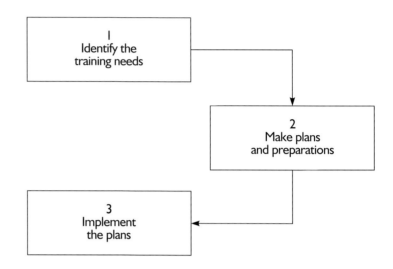

This stage requires Gwyneth to:

■ put the plans into practice;
■ ensure the training is carried out, keeping in mind individual needs and individual capabilities;
■ be flexible in the approach to training and methods of learning;
■ be patient and avoid judging learners too harshly;
■ monitor progress carefully and be prepared to make changes to the plans. No plan will survive reality unaltered.

Activity 12 · 2 mins

Bearing in mind that this is a cycle we are completing and that the last stage must link back to stage 1, what do you think the final stage of this cycle is?

_____

_____

_____

The last stage is to **evaluate the programme and feed back the results**. As with all well-run projects and programmes, the 'look back and learn' principle should be applied. Otherwise, how will we be able to do better next time?

6.4 Training cycle stage 4 – Evaluate and feed back the results

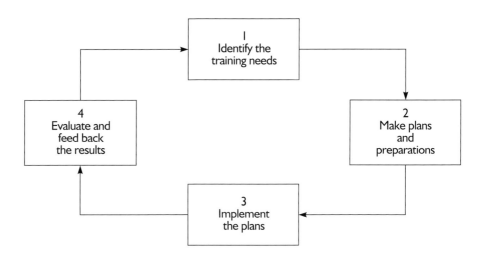

This stage enables Gwyneth to:

- measure the performance of the trainees during training and afterwards;
- check the quality and effectiveness of the training;
- keep training records;
- assess job performance;
- feed back the results to the trainees so they know how well they are progressing;
- note problems and areas of difficulty.

The evaluation and feedback step is invaluable for everyone involved. It is important to those who:

- made the plans and prepared the training;
- gave the training;
- received the training.

Another reason why feedback is so important is that training can never really come to an end in a working environment. There are always new things to learn. People leave and new people join. Others are promoted, creating both opportunities and learning needs.

In the remainder of this workbook we will concentrate on the first two stages in the training cycle. We will look at:

- Identifying training needs (Session B)
- Making training plans (Session C).

Activity 13

2 mins

If we follow the four stages in the order above, what do you expect should happen at the end of stage 4? Tick one of the options.

Option 1   Training should stop   ☐

Option 2   You should go back to stage 1   ☐

Option 3   You should go back to stage 2   ☐

Option 1 isn't correct because training is a continuous requirement. A particular programme to train for a particular need may come to a stop, but there are always new training needs. We should use what we have learned from the evaluation of one training programme or session for the next.

Option 3 (i.e. you finish one lot of training and immediately prepare for the next) assumes that the training needs of your organization have remained the same. This may well not be true, because as time passes circumstances tend to change.

The right answer is Option 2 'Go back to stage 1'.

Learning is for life: you never become 'fully trained'. Each trip around the training cycle presents new learning needs and opportunities.

Self-assessment 1

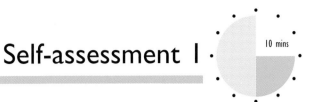

10 mins

1 Complete the following sentences with a suitable word or words chosen from the list below:

DOORS   IMPORTANT   PLANNED   SKILLS
EFFECTIVENESS   KNOWLEDGE   RELEVANT

a Training provides a means of getting _____ and _____

b Training is a _____ procedure designed to improve the

    _____ of people at work.

c For training to be successful trainees may need to be convinced that the

    training is _____ and _____ to them.

d Training opens _____.

2 Training has many benefits – to the organization, to the individual employee and to the manager. List **three** benefits you think are important.

    _____

    _____

    _____

3 Fill in the blanks in the following diagram of the training cycle with suitable words.

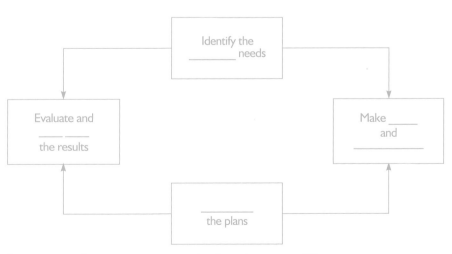

Answers to these questions can be found on page 93.

7 Summary

■ Training provides a means of acquiring skills and knowledge

■ Training is a **planned** procedure designed to improve the effectiveness of people at work.

■ For training to be successful, trainees may need to be **convinced** that the training is relevant and important to them.

■ People who **want** to learn will learn. People who don't, won't.

■ Training benefits the organization, the individual and the manager.

■ The training cycle has four stages and can be represented as follows:

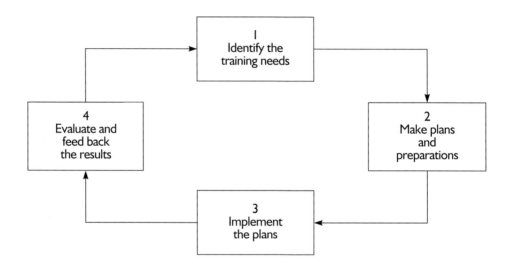

And don't forget that:

■ **Training opens doors.**

Session B
Identifying training needs

1 Introduction

EXTENSIONS I AND 2
Two useful texts which explore training needs analysis in greater depth than we can here.

Before any plans or preparations for training can take place, we have to find out what training is needed. It is important that this is done in an organized and systematic manner. If any errors or wrong diagnoses take place at this stage then the results of the training undertaken will not be those needed or desired by the organization.

There are a number of techniques that can be used to identify accurately what training is required. We will look at some of these techniques in this session. We will also examine the skills that the manager will need to use when employing these techniques. Sometimes the needs will be easy to analyse and determine. In other circumstances it may take skill and patience to discover the precise needs of each workteam member.

For many organizations, identifying training needs is a regular occurrence. Often it can be an annual exercise that follows the business planning process and allows training budgets to be allocated.

The time spent in identifying training needs is time well invested. It will result in training being directed to the areas where it is really needed. It will ensure that the investment made in training is not wasted and that the results are real improvements that make a difference to the operation of the organization.

2 Types of training need

There are three different types of training need:

- organizational;
- workteam;
- individual.

Any training need will be one or another of these.

2.1 Organizational needs

To be fully effective, any analysis of training needs must start with the needs of the whole organization. Some of the key questions of **corporate strategy** that occupy the minds of the top management of any organization are:

- What are the aims of our business?
- What are our strengths and weaknesses?

One of the major strengths or weaknesses of an organization is its workforce. This leads to questions of **personnel planning** such as:

- How well matched is our workforce to the needs of the business?
- What levels of expertise do we have now, and will we need in the future, to achieve our corporate plans?

Organizational needs tend to be defined in broad terms. Many of the objectives need to be broken down and further augmented at a more detailed level before they can be carried out. For many organizational needs this means that they have to be identified at the workteam level.

2.2 Workteam needs

EXTENSION 3
A useful book for developing and training strategy is *Creating a Training and Development Strategy*, by Andrew Mayo.

Each of the levels below top management will normally be expected to participate in corporate strategy at a departmental or workteam level.

Managers of particular departmental functions – such as production, marketing, finance and personnel – will often call upon section heads and workteam managers to identify their training needs in relation to the business objectives set for their department or workteam. These training needs are expected to be established in the light of the defined objectives of the group in question and the specific problems that it has.

Gwyneth Roberts – the manager who had just taken over the general office – decided to talk with her boss about the problems and deficiencies she has recognized.

'There has been so little training done in the past that I hardly know where to begin' she said. 'It's no wonder that the work isn't being done very efficiently.'

Michelle Halliday, Gwyneth's manager nodded. 'I appreciate that things have gone downhill over recent months. Now you have the chance to be the new broom and sweep everything clean. What we need you to do is an assessment of the workteam's training needs. Let's start with short-term problems and then we can gradually start to look at what we'll be needing over a longer period. If you can justify your needs and they fit in with the organization's objectives, I'll talk with my boss to get his backing. I know that higher management are very keen to develop a comprehensive and realistic training programme for the whole organization that is in line with the corporate business plan. But unless we tell them what our problems are – and how training can help to solve them – they may assume our people don't need training.'

Gwyneth left her boss's office wondering where she should start ...

Activity 14

S/NVQ C9.1

This Activity may provide the basis of appropriate evidence for your S/NVQ portfolio. If you are intending to take this course of action, it might be better to write your answers on separate sheets of paper.

Think about your own workteam. What objectives have been set for them recently? What development will they have to undertake in order to meet these objectives?

2.3 Individual needs

Individual training needs will differ greatly depending on the jobs people are doing and the level of skill they possess. Within a workteam of people who are all carrying out the same job, training needs will vary. Some people may already operate and carry out many tasks competently. Other people may have little experience and need to increase their skill and knowledge level. Both these types of people will have training needs but their type and level will differ considerably.

Individual training needs mean just that – they are individual!

Induction training makes new people effective quickly.

There are a number of events which trigger the need for individual training. One is when a new recruit joins the organization.

When someone starts a new job, that person is usually taken through an induction programme. This process of induction for a workteam member would normally be arranged by a first line manager.

Activity 15

3 mins

What's the main purpose of induction for new starters? Jot down a brief answer in the space below.

_____

_____

_____

_____

You may have given a number of different answers, because the process of work induction covers a whole range of topics. In general we would say that:

the main purpose of induction is to make the new starter as effective as possible as quickly as possible.

You will notice that the purpose outlined above is very similar to the definition of training that we gave you earlier. That is not surprising as induction is a form of training. During the first few days or weeks a new starter has to:

- learn about the organization – its history, its products and services, how it is structured, its people and where the new person fits in;
- learn about the rules – the safety rules, what is allowed and what isn't, hours of work, holidays, shift patterns and so on;
- learn about the job – perhaps including a specific job training programme.

Starting a new job is one point in an individual's working life where there is an obvious need for training. But there are a number of others.

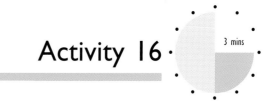

Activity 16   3 mins

Can you think of another point in the working life of the average workteam member where individual training needs are likely to arise?

_____

_____

_____

_____

_____

You may have said that training needs are likely to arise when, for instance, someone:

- moves to a different job, section or department;
- has been selected for promotion;
- has to be instructed in new procedures or safety regulations;
- has been given a new task to carry out;
- is required to cover for another member of the workteam.

In fact we can say that individual training needs arise whenever change occurs.

Because change is continual in modern working life and also because 'refresher' training is necessary from time to time, training is needed throughout the working life of most people.

3 Assessing training needs by analysing jobs

In Session A we introduced you to the idea of using identified **performance gaps** to identify training needs. In order to do this you needed to compare the way your workteam or individual workteam members were actually performing with the way you would like them to perform. This requires you to examine or analyse the actual jobs that they are doing.

One way of looking at this is to think of a pair of scales which we need to balance.

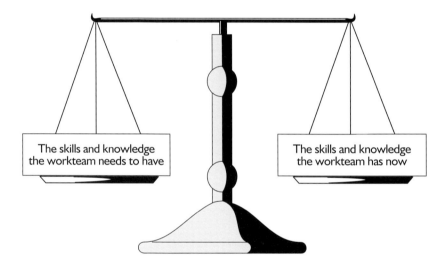

When looking at jobs many organizations now use the standards forming the basis of the Scottish and National Vocational Qualifications (S/NVQs). These standards lay down the required job performance for most recognized occupations and provide an excellent starting point for any organization to compare their own jobs against.

However, because jobs are not always well defined as S/NVQs, and because they tend to change as time goes by, it may be necessary to carry out a little detective work to find out the real training needs of the workteam.

In order to discover the answers to the questions:

■ what activities are comprised in the job – what does the job holder actually do?

- what skills are needed to do the job competently?
- does the job holder have all the skills required?

we may need to:

- refer to any available documentation;
- talk to the job holder or the workteam;
- observe the job holder in action.

Let's look at each of these options in turn.

3.1 Using documentation

Gwyneth decided to find out whether each workteam member was fully trained to carry out their job competently. As she wasn't very familiar with all the work the workteam did, she had to think about the best method of discovering what was involved in each job.

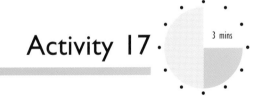

Activity 17

3 mins

What kind of documents might be available in an organization that define what's involved in a particular job? Where are such documents likely to be kept?

_____

_____

_____

Some employees complete diaries or work logs, which could be useful as background information. However, the most useful document to be used here would be found in the personnel department. There you would expect to find a **job description** for every job in the organization.

A job description can be defined as:

A broad statement of the purpose, scope, responsibilities and tasks that constitute a particular job.

A job description is a document that describes the activities carried out by the job holder. It also gives other basic data. The list below gives the typical information likely to be included in a job description:

- job title;
- the line manager to whom the job holder reports;
- the main purpose or function of the job;
- the main tasks or duties involved (these should be only the most important duties to be carried out and ideally should not exceed 12);
- details of the work environment;
- any specific responsibilities;

The job description may also include details of:

- department;
- location;
- name of job holder;
- pay details;
- opportunities for promotion;
- unusual conditions;
- the date the job description was written;
- the name of the writer or analyst.

A job description is a snapshot of a job at a particular moment in time. If it is to be used for training needs analysis purposes it is essential that it is current and accurate.

The following is an example of a job description:

	Job description		
Job title:	IT Information Developer for Migration Project		
Reports to:	IT Manager		
Responsible for:	Trainee Information Developer		
Based at:	Manningham Road IT Centre		
Main role:	To maintain technical and other documentation produced by Migration developers. Documents will include technical functional specifications and any other technical documents produced by Migration Project.		
Key responsibilities and accountabilities:		**% of job (time)**	**Importance**

1 Identify:
  ■ new documents being developed by program developers
  ■ existing documents that need to be updated.
		5%	High

2 Receive final version of each new or updated document from authors, then edit for clarity, consistency, completeness and conformity with house style.		75%	Medium
3 Arrange for appropriate people to review and sign off documents.			
4 Send approved copies of documents, together with signed Quality Review forms, to Configuration Manager for filing.			
5 Manage version control.			
6 Archive signed-off version of documents.			
7 Convert signed-off documents into .pdf format and place on Corporate website.		5%	
8 Inform line manager of instances where a new document will have an impact on an existing document.		10%	
9 Send progress reports to appropriate line manager/s at agreed intervals.			
10 Act as scribe at Quality Review meetings.		5%	Low

11 When requested, provide support to authors in using:
  ■ authoring tools such as MS Word and Visio
  ■ the Migration template.			

From the job description it should be possible to write down the kinds of qualities, skills and knowledge expected of the job holder.

Activity 18

10 mins

Briefly note down the qualities, skills and knowledge that you think might be required from someone taking the job of IT information developer as defined in the job description above.

_____

_____

_____

You might have said that people doing this job should be:

- reliable – because they need to be consistent in checking all documentation which has, or might in the future, change. They are also responsible for reporting regularly on their progress;
- meticulous – because they are responsible for checking that very complicated technical documents are accurate, consistent and complete;
- diplomatic – because they need to build good relationships with the authors whose work they are editing;
- able to work on their own initiative – because they are not working as part of a team, and are not closely managed by their line manager;
- good communicators – as they also have a training role;
- familiar with the appropriate software applications (i.e. MS Word and Visio);
- able to remember complicated facts clearly – because they need to be able to remember the general content of each document.

There are many more skills and qualities which you could have mentioned for a job like this. It would build up to quite a long list.

This statement of the required skills and characteristics (or 'aptitudes') is called a **person profile**, that is it specifies the skills and aptitudes that a person doing that job should have.

By looking carefully at the job description and person profile, you can obtain a good overall understanding of what the job consists of – or at least what it was intended to consist of. You are one step nearer knowing what the training needs are because you now know what you need from the person carrying out this role. Any shortfall from this could be a training need.

However, there are some occasions when it would not be wise to rely entirely on the job description and person profile as your only sources of information about a particular job. Although they are written with the intention of describing the job roles accurately, they may not always do so because:

■ many jobs change over a period of time, and there is often a delay in updating a job description;

■ sometimes the emphasis given in a job description can be rather misleading when it comes to assessing training needs. For example the job description for the information developer emphasised the tasks relating to editing and reviewing the new documents, but one of the most difficult skills to master in such a job is template management – which has only been given a low priority.

3.2 Using discussion

Keep people informed about what you are doing and why.

When discussing training needs with a job holder the first thing to inform them about is **what** you are doing and **why**. You will need their involvement and co-operation to proceed and so it is vital to gain their commitment at this stage.

You may choose to have this discussion with the workteam or privately with each individual. However you choose to carry out the discussion you will need to ensure that the information you receive is of the right quality and quantity. To do this you will need to adopt a constructive questioning approach.

To ask constructive questions you will need to ask **open** questions. These are questions that people cannot answer with just a 'yes' or a 'no'. They require them to give some information and join in a discussion. Open questions are very useful for establishing rapport, opening up topics or discovering feelings. Very often this type of question will begin with the words:

■ What?
■ Where?
■ Why?
■ Who?
■ When?
■ How?

You might ask questions like:

What activities take up most of your working day?
What ideas have you got about . . .?
How do you feel about . . .?

3.3 Observing the job holder

The next obvious step, if you are still in doubt about what is involved in the job, is to observe the job holder in action.

This can be done formally or informally.

■ **Formal observations**

This would happen if you put aside a set period of time, perhaps a day or so, and sit or stand near to the job holder and watch what tasks are performed. While watching you would also make notes of what you see.

■ **Informal observations**

As part of the normal routine you will usually observe your workteam in action. You can therefore observe them over a period of time without seeming to do so. You should not take notes when you are observing informally.

Activity 19 · 3 mins

Can you think of **one** advantage and **one** disadvantage for each method of observing the job holder?

Formal observation:

_____

_____

Informal observation:

_____

_____

If you are observing people formally some of the advantages are that it allows you to discuss the process with the job holder and explain the reasons for carrying out the observation. The job holder is then able to prepare him/herself for the event. It also enables you to put aside set time to carry out the observation.

Some of the disadvantages are that people do not always behave normally when they are being watched – they may feel that they should do what they're expected to do, rather than what they usually do. Another problem is that it may arouse feelings of resentment.

You may have mentioned some of the following advantages of observing informally. It allows managers to spread the time needed for the task of observation over a period of time and it also allows them to get more involved with the work of the workteam.

Some disadvantages of this method, however, are that is it not such a systematic approach and thus may not be so accurate. Managers may also find themselves distracted from the task by other events and so not accomplish it.

Observation allows managers to analyse a task because it allows them to see it actually being carried out. It also allows managers to assess the competence of the person carrying out the job. This can be extremely useful when analysing training needs.

4 Training needs analysis by task

In order to specify training needs very precisely, it may be worthwhile analysing jobs task by task.

> Gwyneth, in her efforts to identify the training needs of the workteam:
>
> - read the job descriptions very carefully;
> - talked to each member of the workteam in some depth about what they actually did, what they needed to know and what skills they felt they were lacking;
> - observed them in action over a period of time and learned as much as she could about the workteam's duties and activities.
>
> At the end of all this, she felt that she understood the training needs of most workteam members and she took steps to get the appropriate training organized.
>
> However, there was still one job that she was uncertain about – that of the receptionist, Debbie Wilson. Debbie worked alone, outside the main office, and so it wasn't so easy for Gwyneth to observe her in

action. Gwyneth decided she would have to sit down with Debbie for a period and record what she did and how well she did it. She would then list every task that Debbie carried out.

Gwyneth used the following chart to record her findings.

Task Analysis Assessment Chart		
Job title	**Receptionist**	
Job holder	**Debbie Wilson**	
Task description	*Knowledge/Skill Required*	*Proficiency reached and training advised*
Task 1: **Dealing with visitors**	Skill in dealing with callers, trades people, job applicants etc.	Carried out efficiently. No further training required at this time.
Task 2: **Operating the telephone switchboard**	Skill in handling callers, knowledge of and skills at operating switchboard, knowledge of organizational procedures in handling callers.	Job holder not fully conversant with new switchboard operation – training needed. Not familiar with procedures for handling difficult callers – instruction needed (if procedures exist).
Task 3: **Operating the computer to access status of stock figures for organizational sales staff**	Skills in and knowledge of computer inputting and interpreting display.	Does a reasonable job in spite of lack of training. Background training in system operation would aid understanding.
Task 4: **Typing when not busy**	Skills in typing.	Not very good. Job holder is not a trained typist. External training could be recommended but frequent interruptions mean this aspect of the job may have to be re-evaluated.

When she studied the receptionist's job Gwyneth in fact found out more information than simply the training needed. For one thing, she learned that Task 3 on the chart above (using a computer) did not appear on the job description. The reason for this was that this was a recently introduced task and the personnel department had not yet updated the document.

Activity 20

3 mins

Can you spot one other point which appears in the chart above which was perhaps both very surprising and was very useful information to the organization?

_____

_____

_____

You may have noticed two points. One was the fact that no instructions had been given about the way to handle 'difficult' telephone callers, which probably means that no such instructions existed.

The other point was that Task 4 (typing when not busy) needed to be re-evaluated because Debbie was not a skilled typist and had so many interruptions that it is doubtful whether she could have done a good job in any case. Training was feasible here but not a very practical solution to the problem.

Activity 21

15 mins

S/NVQ C9.1

This Activity may provide the basis of appropriate evidence for your S/NVQ portfolio. If you are intending to take this course of action, it might be better to write your answers on separate sheets of paper.

You may like to try your hand at analysing a job using our chart. For this activity pick a job that you are very familiar with but that is also one that you know you will be required to arrange some training for in the near future. List **three** or **four** tasks that are included in the job and summarize the **skills** and the **knowledge** required for each task. Then make a judgement about how well the task is being performed and suggest any training you feel would help the job holder in performing the task better.

Task Analysis Assessment Chart		
Job title		
Job holder		
Task description	Knowledge/skill required	Proficiency reached and training advised
Task 1:		
Task 2:		
Task 3:		
Task 4:		

You may not have found this activity too easy to do. In a real-life situation, you may spend quite some time analysing a particular job before you feel you can properly assess the training needs. And, of course, training needs analysis is not something you do once and forget about.

A workteam either develops or stagnates.

It isn't usually a question of 'clearing up all the training needs' and then forgetting all about training. Training never stops. Once you've identified the needs of your workteam and instituted one training programme you will probably find yourself having to think about the next lot of training. Don't forget that a workteam either develops or stagnates.

Training is one way to help your workteam continue to develop.

5 Other training needs identification techniques

The remainder of this session will explore other ways of identifying and agreeing training needs.

5.1 Versatility charts

Coping with unexpected absence is a problem nearly every manager has to deal with from time to time. It may be caused by a temporary absence like sickness, but it may be of a more permanent nature, like an employee suddenly leaving.

A manager who can cope without too many difficulties in this kind of situation probably has a well-organized and well-trained workteam. Having the capacity to deal with absence depends upon:

- good communications and a good record-keeping system, so that the workteam and the manager are not too reliant on information that is only carried around in the head of the absentee;
- having people trained to do more than one job.

What about training? How can a manager be sure that there is enough cross-training among workteam members so that absenteeism won't normally result in an unacceptable level of disruption?

The easy way to find out is to make a versatility chart that shows who's trained in what. In simple terms a versatility chart is an employee/job matrix which lists all the individuals from a workteam across the top of a grid and lists all the main departmental tasks down the side. Against each name the manager can mark the tasks that each individual is able to perform using a code such as the following:

M   main person normally undertaking this task
S   person required to stand in
C   person is competent to carry out the task

Gwyneth's workteam consisted of eight people, seven of whom worked in the General Office. Felix was her Chief Clerk and he had been with the workteam the longest. Gwyneth realized that if Felix went sick there would be no-one to cover for him. She decided she had better make a summary of which workteam members were trained to do what jobs. She drew up the following versatility chart.

Versatility Chart							
	General Office Staff						
	Jean	Felix	Martha	Aracea	Cathy	Eddie	Max
Wages		S C		S C	S C	M C	S C
Purchase ledger		S C		M C			
Sales ledger			S C	S C	M C		
Stock control	S C		M C	S C	S C	S C	M C
Work allocation		M C					
Control and checking		M C					
Customer complaints		M C	S C				
Payment authorization		M C					
Customer enquiries		S C	M C			S C	
Data input	S C	S C	S C	M C	M C	S C	M C
General admin	M C	S C	S C	S C	S C	S C	S C
Word processing	M C						

To complete the final estimate with the versatility chart Gwyneth will need to calculate the following.

a How many people carry out this job competently at the present time?
b How many competent people are required with skills in this area to ensure adequate cover?
c How many people are currently competent to stand in for this task?

The number of people requiring training, which we will call (d), is worked out as follows:

b − a + c = d

Activity 22

5 mins

Using the information provided below work out (d), the number of people who require training in each task. Sometimes the calculation will produce a minus figure (see Wages). That means there are more than enough people to cover the task and the number requiring training is zero.

Training Required				
	Calculation			
Task	a	b	c	d
Wages	1	2	4	0 (−3)
Purchase ledger	1	3	1	
Sales ledger	1	3	2	
Stock control	2	4	5	
Work allocation	1	2	0	
Control and checking	1	2	0	
Customer complaints	1	2	1	
Payment authorization	1	2	0	
Customer enquiries	1	4	2	
Data input	3	5	4	
General admin	1	4	6	
Word processing	1	3	0	

Answers to this Activity can be found on page 95.

You will see that it's possible to tell quite a lot from a simple versatility chart. The chart is easy to draw up and very useful when it comes to rearranging cover for different job functions.

Of course it won't tell the manager who to train to cover for the necessary tasks. That will be a matter of considering things such as:

- the present workload of the employees;
- their existing skill levels;
- their ability to learn new tasks;
- their willingness to learn new tasks.

Activity 23

S/NVQ C9.1

This Activity may provide the basis of appropriate evidence for your S/NVQ portfolio. If you are intending to take this course of action, it might be better to write your answers on separate sheets of paper.

Complete the versatility chart below for your workteam or section.

Versatility Chart							
Jobs or tasks	Workteam or section member						

Once you have completed the versatility chart you will now be able to decide which tasks or jobs require additional cover.

Training Required				
Task	Calculation			
	a	b	c	d

You will now be able to decide who should undertake the training required to make this additional cover available. A chart is provided below to assist you with this task.

It may be that you will need to refer to your manager before you can make any recommendations and you will certainly need to talk to the job holders themselves. A column is included on the form for you to identify further discussion required.

Training Recommendation Form		
Workteam member's name	Training recommended	Details of discussions required

Although versatility charts are often useful, they do not always give a complete picture of training needs.

Activity 24 · 3 mins

Can you think of one work situation where a versatility chart would **not** tell a manager everything he or she needs to know about workteam training needs?

_____

_____

_____

Versatility charts don't tell you about the training needs beyond the normal job functions of the workteam.

- Safety training, for example, may require a completely separate training programme.
- Versatility charts assume that one task consists of skills that can be learned in a reasonably short period of time by another workteam member. This is by no means always true. Some skills can only be learned after years of practice.
- They don't allow for the range of skills and knowledge that one job might encompass, nor do they give any indication of the degree of expertise required by the job holder.

5.2 Diff-rating scales

A diff-rating scale works by specifying tasks and rating them according to whether you consider them to be:

- important;
- carried out frequently;
- difficult to learn.

This scale should help you to decide which training should be given priority. Here is an example of a diff-rating scale.

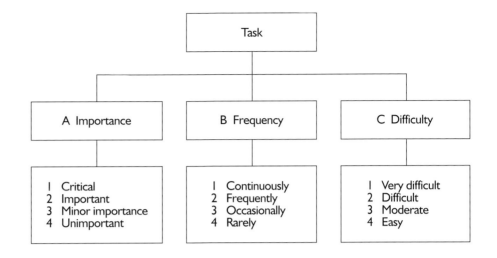

It is possible to take a task and to give it a rating of 1 to 4 for each of the three categories A, B and C.

Activity 25

5 mins

What training recommendations would you make for the following tasks that have been given the following ratings?

Task	Rating	Training recommendation
Task 1	A4, B4, C4	
Task 2	A1, B1, C1	
Task 3	A1, B4, C4	
Task 4	A1, B4, C1	

■ **Task 1**

This task does not require any training as it is unimportant and rarely carried out. It is also easy to learn and should be picked up when needed without any specific training.

■ **Task 2**

This task needs immediate training as it is a critical task and one that is carried out continuously. It is, however, very difficult to learn and this will need to be taken into account when planning the training.

■ **Task 3**

Training should be undertaken in this example as it is a critical activity. However, as it is rarely carried out, a one-off training session may not suffice and regular refresher training may be needed. This should not be too difficult to arrange as the task is an easy one to learn.

■ **Task 4**

Immediate training should be arranged for this task as again it is a critical activity. However, the planning will need to take into account the fact that it is not an easy task to learn and that it is rarely used at work. This means that lots of practice will not be available at work and will need to be included in the training.

5.3 Appraisal interviews

Another method used to identify training needs is the formal performance appraisal interview which provides a useful opportunity to discuss training needs with an individual. It gives workteam members the chance to say what training they think they need or would like. It also gives managers an opportunity to explain what training is available or is planned.

Performance appraisal is a method of evaluating a workteam member's progress and performance. It is usually conducted as part of an annual formal interview.

In many companies employees are encouraged to prepare for this interview by completing a pre-appraisal questionnaire. This makes them think about such issues as:

■ self-assessment of past performance;
■ strengths and weaknesses;
■ areas for improvement in the future;
■ key objectives for the next year;
■ ambitions for the future;
■ training needs.

The employee is then able to participate more actively in the interview.

At the interview, both parties exchange information regarding the job and the workteam member's progress. At the end of the interview a summary is written, including agreed future objectives for the person concerned. A record of training needs should also be included on the summary document.

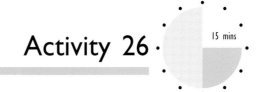

Activity 26

15 mins

S/NVQ C9.1

This Activity may provide the basis of appropriate evidence for your S/NVQ portfolio. If you are intending to take this course of action, it might be better to write your answers on separate sheets of paper.

Obtain a copy of your organization's performance appraisal documentation and list below the areas that it covers. What details does it contain about training needs? Blank forms will give you some information but completed appraisal documents will give you more insight into the process. However, you must obtain the permission of the people to whom the appraisals relate and, if they allow you to use them, remove all names and other personal information that could identify them. Make sure that they do have identified training needs on them.

_____

_____

_____

_____

_____

_____

_____

_____

You can learn more about appraising performance in *Appraising Performance* in this series.

6 Agreeing and recording identified training needs

It is an important part of your role to identify accurate training needs. However, the task is not completed at this stage. The training needs must be agreed and approved, perhaps by both your line manager and the individuals in question. Having reached agreement it is then essential for the agreement to be recorded. This will allow you to move on to the next stage in the training cycle – that of planning and preparing for the training.

6.1 Agreeing training needs

We mentioned above that it is possible that two different people will need to be consulted to agree training needs.

■ **The workteam member**

In Session A we said that the commitment and motivation of individuals is essential if training is to be effective. This means that the individuals need to recognize the need for the identified training. For this recognition to occur you will need to discuss training needs with the individual. We have already suggested that discussion is one way of identifying training needs anyway, but this discussion may need to be held after you have reached some conclusions.

The discussion will also enable you to talk over with the individuals any personal circumstances or special learning requirements they may have.

Activity 27

15 mins

S/NVQ C9.1

This Activity may provide the basis of appropriate evidence for your S/NVQ portfolio. If you are intending to take this course of action, it might be better to write your answers on separate sheets of paper.

Can you think of an example of when a discussion about training needs with one of your workteam has resulted in you modifying your recommendations for training? Give details below.

Ask the employee involved to sign a statement to say that this is a true record of what took place.

_____

_____

_____

_____

■ **Your line manager**

There may be several occasions when you might need to refer to a higher level of management for guidance on analysing training needs. For example you might need to talk about:

■ information on organizational or workteam objectives;
■ details of training budgets available;
■ guidance on stand-in cover requirements;
■ policy on techniques to use when identifying training needs;
■ advice on problems encountered.

If you are compiling an S/NVQ portfolio, and have a specific example of when you have needed guidance, write a record of the circumstances and ask the manager involved to sign it. You may then be able use this as testimony evidence.

6.2 Recording training needs

Once agreement has been reached the next step is to record that agreement. There is no set way of doing this, although it is important that it is in writing.

52

A short memo, letter or report giving details of the final decisions arrived at is all that is needed before moving on to the planning and preparation stage.

In this session we have given you three examples of ways in which training needs can be recorded:

■ a task analysis assessment chart as used in Activity 21
■ the training recommendation form used with the versatility chart in Activity 23
■ the performance appraisal documentation discussed in Activity 26.

This concludes the task of identifying training needs and allows the record to be passed on to the relevant personnel. We can now start stage 2 of the training cycle in Session C.

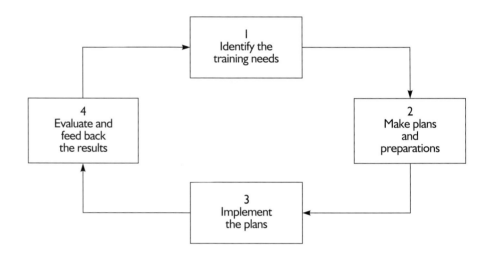

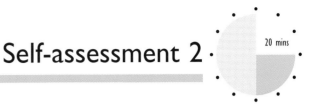

Self-assessment 2

20 mins

Complete the crossword below using the clues given.

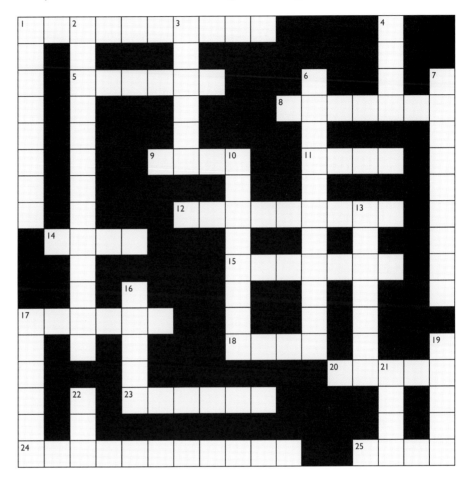

Across

1 One of the three types of training need. (10)
5 Training will always be needed when this is happening. (6)
8 If workteams don't do this they will stagnate. (7)
9 Training needs may affect the whole work ----. (4)
11 Training needs analysis is a systematic method and should be completed ---- by step. (4)
12 The training at the beginning. (9)
14 Versatility charts show the ---- person normally undertaking a task and the person required to stand in. (4)
15 and 4 down It is important that managers ------- what the ---- benefits of training are. (7, 4)
17 The question that it's OK to say no to. (6)
18 See 3 down. (4)
20 When being observed formally some job holders ----- in a resentful way. (5)
23 When analysing jobs and tasks it is important to look at both ------ and knowledge. (6)
24, and 1 and 16 down Part of the ----------- job is to -------- training -----. (11, 8, 5)
25 Because of organizational needs it is not always possible to give individuals the training they ----. (4)

Down

1 See 24 across. (8)
2 The job description is this. (13)
3 and 10, and 18 across Diff-rating scales work by rating the ------ of difficulty in a task. Tasks are rated as very difficult, difficult, -------- or ----. (6, 8, 4)
4 See 15 across. (4)
6 and 17 The matrices that help identify training needs. (11, 6)
7 The annual interview that monitors progress. (9)
10 See 3 down. (8)
13 and 21 You should try to ------- job holders in their own ---- of work. (7, 4)
16 See 24 across. (5)
17 See 6 down. (6)
19 It's important at the ----- of the identification process to decide what methods are to be used. (5)
21 See 13 down. (4)
22 The performance --- identifies the training need. (3)

Answers to this crossword can be found on page 94.

7 Summary

- Training needs arise from three sources: **organizational** needs, **workteam** needs and **individual** needs.

- Training needs can be **analysed** by:

  - referring to any available documentation, including job descriptions;
  - talking to job holders;
  - watching the job holder in action;
  - carrying out a formal performance appraisal interview.

- Individual training needs arise whenever **change** takes place.

- Training is one way to help your workteam continue to **develop**.

- **Training needs identification techniques** include:

  - job analysis;
  - task analysis;
  - versatility charts;
  - diff-rating scales;
  - performance appraisal interviews.

Session C
Planning successful training

1 Introduction

EXTENSION 4
For help in designing clear training objectives and much more, read *How to Write and Prepare Training Materials.*

As with so many management activities **planning** is the key to success.

This is certainly true of training. To be effective it must be carefully thought out in a logical and clear way. At the beginning we need to have clear objectives. We need to have a precise understanding of what we are trying to achieve. Once we are clear about this we can then start looking at the details of the training.

We need to look carefully at the training methods to be used and to consider which methods would assist with the learning. We also need to plan the content of the programme to ensure that it is logical and sequential and that the most important elements are included. All the administrative arrangements must be carried out to ensure facilities, equipment, materials and trainees are available. And finally we need to plan the way in which we aim to evaluate the effectiveness of the final result.

Induction training is a good example of training that needs to be well planned. A new employee's introduction to the organization needs to contain everything that the person will need to know in order to settle down quickly and fit in. It is not something that will just happen, nor will it be complete and interesting if it is not planned.

During this session we will look at each of these issues in turn.

2 What are we trying to achieve?

When drawing up plans and projects, it's best to start at the end.

What we mean by this apparently paradoxical statement is that any plan or project must have a purpose (or end) and, until you are clear about what you are trying to achieve, you can't expect to succeed.

What's more, before you start, you need to know how to **measure** the success of your venture. Otherwise, it may be difficult to know whether it has succeeded.

To do this thoroughly you need a defined method of measurement. Writing training objectives will provide you with this necessary measure.

When writing objectives it is important that they conform to the SMART principle. This states that objectives should be:

```
S  pecific
M  easurable
A  chievable
R  elevant
T  ime bound
```

■ Specific

Training objectives must be precise and exact in explaining what is to be achieved. This means that the specific objectives of a particular training programme must be defined in terms of the desired improvement in work performance. Specific objectives should describe both **performance** and **standards**, i.e. what is to be done and how well it is to be done.

■ Measurable

The purpose of setting objectives is to enable some measurement of success to take place. This means that objectives must be written in terms that are easy and possible to measure.

■ **Achievable**

Objectives should only state what it is reasonable to expect the trainee to achieve. It would not, for example, be realistic to expect someone to pass a driving test after just one lesson. This could not be achieved in the time scale. Again, if the necessary resources were not available, the objective would not be achievable.

■ **Relevant**

The training objectives set must be relevant both to the work the trainees are carrying out and to the training content of the programme. There is no point in teaching someone spreadsheets if they are only going to be involved in word processing.

■ **Time bound**

Training objectives should clearly state the time in which the trainee is expected to achieve the desired results. If the programme is a one-week course are they expected to achieve the results at the end of that time? Will they need further practice? If so, how much longer might this be reasonably expected to take?

Activity 28

Examine the training objectives of the one-day training course below. Decide whether you think they meet the SMART principles.

I   Understand the basic principles of health and safety.   Yes/No

2   Conduct health and safety audits to meet the standards of the Health and Safety Executive.   Yes/No

3   At the next team meeting explain clearly their management responsibilities under the Health and Safety at Work Act.   Yes/No

4   Draw up an accurate plan of their area of work showing where all fire exits and fire extinguishers are located in readiness for the next safety committee meeting.   Yes/No

Objectives 3 and 4 are both good objectives. They are specific, measurable, achievable, relevant and time bound.

3 The way people learn

Why is it that some things you are told just don't stick, yet other things which are useful or important to you are there for life as soon as you have learned them?

3.1 Participative learning methods

Compare these two learning situations.

1   You are attending a lecture on a subject that doesn't really interest you and that doesn't seem to be very relevant to what you do at work.

2   You are taking part in a discussion with an expert on a topic which has a great deal of bearing on your everyday work activities and which you find very interesting.

The main differences between these two learning situations are that:

■   the subject of the lecture **is not relevant** to what you do but the subject of the discussion is.
■   the subject of the lecture **does not interest you** but the subject of the discussion does.
■   the lecture is a passive training situation that **you are not able to get involved in** apart from listening, but you can **take an active part in** the discussion.

In these circumstances you are more likely to learn from the discussion than from the lecture.

This illustrates three important principles of learning:

> **People learn better when they:**
>
> ■ **can relate what they are studying to something they already know and understand;**
> ■ **are interested in the subject being taught;**
> ■ **take part actively in the learning process, rather than simply listening or watching passively.**

Activity 31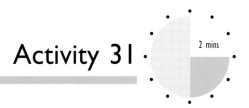

2 mins

Imagine you are instructing members of your workteam about a new job. It is important that the workteam members learn and remember certain information.

Tick **one** box to show whether you think it would it be better to:

■ collect the information yourself and present it to the workteam members or ☐

■ get them to find out the information for themselves. ☐

From the learning point of view, it would be far better to encourage the workteam members to seek out the information for themselves because:

People learn better when they discover information for themselves rather than being presented with it.

3.2 Learning styles

When learning any new piece of knowledge or skill a learner needs to go through four separate stages (rather like the training cycle). These stages make up the learning cycle, which can be illustrated as follows.

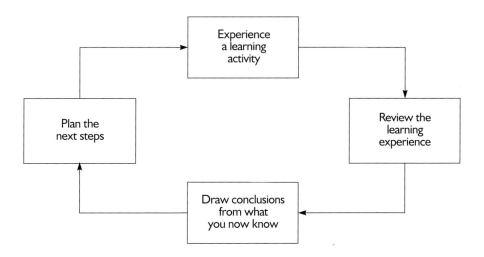

Although there is no best way of learning it is possible for the trainee to join the learning cycle at any stage and learners usually have one (or possibly two) stages within the learning cycle where they prefer to start. These stages are their preferred **styles of learning**. Let's look at four trainees with different preferred styles of learning.

Stephen Bryant likes to learn in an active way – he likes to learn by doing. He is not afraid of making mistakes and will try anything once. He has an 'activist' style of learning.

Jean Walsh likes to stand back and think about things before she tries them out. She likes to collect information and data and carefully analyse it before she applies it in practice. She has a 'reflector' style.

Graham James likes to adapt information gained and put it into sound logical theories. He likes to gather facts together, and is keen on basic principles and models. He needs to be given the basic theories before he can start to think about how they can be applied in practice. He has a 'theorist' style.

Margaret Hill is a very practical person who likes to try out ideas and theories to see how they work in practice. She needs to take ideas and then plan how they can be applied before she actually tries them out. She has a 'pragmatist' style.

Activity 32 · 5 mins

Consider two members of your own workteam. What preferred styles of learning do you think they have and what are the reasons for your choice? Record your answers in the space provided.

Workteam member	Learning style preferred	Reasons

Once you have identified the learning styles of individuals, what should you do about it? Well, it might affect the training methods you plan to use. For example a theorist might prefer a more formal training session, whereas an activist might prefer some practical training.

4 Training on or off the job?

Both on-the-job training and off-the-job training have advantages and disadvantages. They can usefully be combined to create a comprehensive training programme.

4.1 Training on the job

One common approach to job training is the 'sit by Nellie' method. You probably know the kind of thing.

'Oh, you must be the new starter. Here, come and sit by Nellie for a few days. She'll show you the ropes.' And Nellie, being a patient and kind person and used to 'showing the ropes' to trainees, tries her best to pass on her skills and knowledge. At least we hope she does.

In truth, if the job really is simple and can be learned quickly by most people then the 'sit by Nellie' system often works well enough. Otherwise it does have its drawbacks.

Activity 33

3 mins

Can you think of **two** disadvantages to the 'sit by Nellie' approach to training?

_____

_____

_____

There are a number of disadvantages, even if Nellie enjoys being used in this way and makes every effort to be a good trainer.

- Nellie may not have received any formal training herself, either in the job or in the skills of training.
- The 'watch me do this' method can omit any explanation to the trainee about the underlying principles involved.
- The training may be unstructured, not planned and not prepared.
- An unskilled trainer may pass on bad habits as well as good ones.
- The 'pool of knowledge' in the workteam may diminish after time because of a lack of fresh ideas and a dilution of skills.
- Mistakes made can be very costly.

Mistakes can be very costly.

You probably came up with still more drawbacks to the system.

If you are currently using the 'sit by Nellie' approach you may want to ask yourself if you can improve the learning techniques but still allow trainees to learn on the job.

Activity 34  5 mins

What circumstances need to be present in an on-the-job training programme to ensure its success? Try to list at least **three** things.

_____

_____

_____

_____

Some of the circumstances you may have mentioned are these.

- The people undertaking the training should themselves be trained, not only in the job but also in training skills.
- There should be a structured, planned and prepared training programme, which includes some explanation about the underpinning knowledge and theories.
- A number of different trainers need to be involved in the training.
- Adequate time must be built into the programme for practice.

Well-planned and well-prepared on-the-job training takes a lot of time to organize if it is to be done well. But it can also result in excellent outcomes. Training provided on the job is often seen as being more relevant and directly related to the job the person is doing.

4.2 Training off the job

Training away from the job also has a number of benefits, such as giving:

- a better chance to think clearly and to concentrate away from the noise and the bustle of the workplace;
- freedom from interruption and from the pressures of work;
- an opportunity to practise where it does not matter if mistakes are made;
- an opportunity to think through the principles behind actions and perhaps to question why the work is done in the way it is.

As with on-the-job training there are some disadvantages with this method of training. Off-the-job training requires people to be away from work for periods of time, it requires the provision of training facilities such as a room and flipchart, and it often has to rely on simulation-type practice.

5 Choosing the best method

There are numerous methods of training. Your choice will depend on:

- the needs of your trainee(s);
- the demands of your task;
- the constraints of your budget;
- the resources you have available.

This section will introduce some of the more commonly used techniques so that you can decide which ones you would like to build in at the planning stage. In the workbook entitled *Delivering Training* we will look at these techniques more closely and explore delivering training using some of these methods.

Some methods, such as demonstrations, will normally take place at work, but on the whole these methods can be used flexibly in the workplace or away from the immediate pressure of the job.

■ Demonstrations

The purpose of a demonstration is to pass on skills by imitation and practice. It differs from the 'sit by Nellie' approach in that it is planned, and is combined with clear explanations of what's involved and the reasons behind the actions.

The procedure is best carried out in the following four stages:

■ preparation
■ introduction
■ demonstration and explanation
■ practice.

■ Coaching

Coaching is sometimes thought of as an extension of the demonstration technique already described. However, it is also a process of developing the experience and abilities of partially trained individuals through:

■ issuing specific, planned tasks that are assessed on completion;
■ continuously monitoring and appraising progress;
■ holding regular review sessions.

■ Presentations and discussions

A presentation is a prepared speech, and is usually followed by discussions on specific topics.

Presentations are a way of imparting information to a group rather than simply to individuals. They can be used for a variety of purposes besides giving direct job instructions, for example, for conveying news about the organization.

The idea of a discussion is to get a group of people actively participating in learning.

■ Videos and DVDs

You may have access to training videos or DVDs. These can be very helpful training aids, provided they are well made and relevant.

Their main advantage is that, as the saying goes, 'a picture can be worth a thousand words'. It is possible to show on video or DVD what cannot otherwise be seen, perhaps showing a process in slow motion or an interview or appraisal situation which would normally take place in private.

One disadvantage is that they can quickly become out of date.

The best way to use videos and DVDs is to combine them with another form of training. It's a good idea to hold a discussion session immediately after a video showing, in order to review and reinforce ideas.

■ **Mentoring**

A mentor is a person who agrees to act as an adviser or guide to a person with less experience than themselves. The general aim is to help the inexperienced person to develop his or her long-term goals.

■ **Open/flexible learning**

We shouldn't forget the method you are using for training at the moment – open/flexible learning.

Open/flexible learning has several advantages, assuming you can find a course suitable to your needs. These advantages include:

■ working at your own pace, in your own time and wherever suits you best;
■ interactive design, so that you can respond to questions and activities and are given feedback and analysis.
■ the frequent use of printed materials, which are easily portable and accessible anywhere, relatively cheap and may be preferred by some users to working on screen.

■ **Computer-based learning (CBL)**

Computer-based learning is a type of open learning in which the information is displayed on a computer screen rather than on paper. The training is normally interactive, i.e. the program contains information, case studies, assessment tests, etc. and learners are able to input responses via their keyboards.

The main formats are as follows.

■ Computer-based training (CBT) packages – These are interactive learning programs which contain text, diagrams and, often, audio and video. They provide information, interactive exercises, assessment and feedback. CBT programs can be loaded onto a pc from the Internet, from the organization's own intranet, a CD-ROM disk or, increasingly in the future, from a DVD tape.

   The benefits of CBT include the fact that it is usually developed in a modular format, i.e. the subject matter is presented in separate modules that can be studied alone or as part of a series and, from which either the trainer or the learner can select the topics required for a particular course. The learners can learn at a time convenient to them, and take as long as they need. Possible drawbacks are that they will need a pc, and some people find that they become isolated and demotivated if they are not working in a group. Again, unless you can arrange for tutorial support to be provided, there is no one to ask if things go wrong.

■ Online reference manuals – reference documents, such as operations manuals, can be accessed online in .pdf format by anyone who has Adobe Acrobat Reader software on their pc. Again, this format is not interactive.

■ PowerPoint presentations – these are useful for displaying diagrams and other important points for a presentation. They can be delivered to learners via the organisation's intranet or displayed from the computer onto a wall screen by means of a projector. They are not interactive, i.e. the learner cannot key in information, select options from a menu or answer on-screen assessment questions.

6 Designing and using visual aids

Any training session can be made more visual and thus more interesting by using visual aids. There are a large number of aids available to you. In this section we have selected a few of the most commonly used ones. We will give you some more information on, and examine the uses of, the following:

■ overhead projectors
■ overhead transparencies
■ flipcharts
■ handouts.

6.1 Overhead projectors

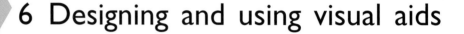

Overhead projectors (OHPs) can be invaluable training aids. They are used to display text or graphics from a transparency (OHT) onto a large screen fixed to the wall. In this way the information is magnified and it is possible for a larger number of people to view the information.

The transparency is placed on a glass plate on the OHP and a strong light is shone through it from below to reflect the image via a mirror onto the screen.

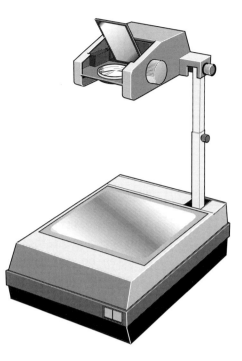

Before using the OHP it is important for you to be familiar with the way it works. You must ensure that:

- the projector is working, is clean and that there is a spare bulb;
- the projector is properly focused so that the image is clear;
- the image is directly projected onto the screen and that it fits the space available;
- the trainees can clearly see the screen.

There are a few simple rules to follow when you are using the OHP that will help your presentation to look more professional and proficient. These rules are as follows.

- Place the transparency onto the machine first and then switch the machine on.
- Always face the trainees. Do not turn around to look at the screen.
- Have a paper copy of the information on your transparency in front of you.
- Point to the transparency on the projector, not to the projection on the screen.
- Switch off the machine when the information is finished with.
- Only remove transparencies from the projector after it has been switched off. This is to avoid blurring and distorting the images.

It is also possible to project images onto a screen using a computer presentation system. This is a computerized version of the OHP and has the added advantage of allowing you to prepare or alter images instantly on the computer screen.

- make sure that the handout is well spaced out and not full of writing – use plenty of white space;
- give the handout a title (and date of the latest version);
- use diagrams and graphics where these would be helpful;
- use different letter sizing, bold print, underlining, etc.

7 Planning the training

Let's assume that you have decided on:

- the objectives of the training programme;
- methods of participative learning and learning styles;
- location of the training;
- training methods;
- visual aids.

Planning well means getting the detail right. To complete the planning of your training there are still a few items that need to be considered. In this section we will look at the finishing touches that will ensure your training programme can be delivered effectively. These are:

- course content and order of presentation;
- timing;
- facilities and equipment.

7.1 Course content

The content of the course will depend on your organization and the needs of your workteam. If we take the induction course as an example, you would normally include such topics as: company rules, health and safety rules, location of fire exits, fire drills, a company tour, introductions to other staff, pay details, pension rights, holiday entitlement, car parking, training available and details of the job.

You may find that you need to:

- revise your own knowledge and understanding of the subject (you will probably find that you learn a lot more when you come to do the training; trying to teach something is an excellent way of learning it);

- break down the material into manageable chunks;
- go through things stage by stage, bearing in mind what the trainees do and do not know;
- work out how you are going to explain difficult points;
- plan the stages at which you will summarise the main points and assess the trainees' understanding of what they have learned so far.

Don't forget that trainees may need help with the basics – how to do simple calculations, help with written and spoken English, and so on. They may also need help and encouragement to learn in order to overcome any fears they may have. In some instances they may even need to learn how to learn.

At this stage you will find it invaluable to prepare a **training plan**. This will help you to organize each training session, provide a structure for you to follow, and act as a memory jogger during the training session.

Timing	Content	Method	Visual aids
10.00	Introduce self and trainees	Pairs exercise	
10.15	Introduction and purpose of topic	Tutor input Question/Answer	OHT 1
10.30	HSWA 1974 S.2	Tutor input	OHT 2 Handout
	Exercise: 'What does this mean to you'	Group work. Spokesperson to report back	

7.2 Timing

A number of decisions must be made with regard to the timing of the training. For example:

- total length of time to be given to the training;
- duration of each session (for example, three hours);
- frequency of sessions (for example, one session on each of five consecutive days, one day a week for five weeks, etc.).

You may also need to give some thought to how you will cope with the trainees' absence and who will cover for them at work.

7.3 Facilities and equipment

It is obviously important to make sure that all the equipment is available and in working order. There's little joy in spending weeks in preparing a programme only to discover that a vital piece of equipment isn't working or that another group has planned a course in the same place on the same day.

You will need to check that the following are available and, where appropriate, booked:

- trainers;
- trainees;
- training rooms;
- training aids such as OHPs, flipcharts, videos, tables, chairs;
- computers;
- appropriate training software and training databases;
- simulation equipment;
- refreshments.

Activity 36

20 mins

Go back to Activity 29 and look at the objectives that you wrote for the new induction programme for your team.

Taking just one of the objectives, complete the training plan for it below, keeping in mind all you have learned so far.

Timing	Content	Method	Visual aids

8 Conforming to legislative requirements

When giving information to trainees about legislation, codes of practice and good practice guides it is essential to ensure that your information is accurate and up to date. For example, an induction course would need to include information on health and safety, together with the legislation that governs it. This means that you will have to be familiar with such legislation as:

- Health and Safety at Work Act 1974 (HSWA);
- Management of Health and Safety at Work Regulations 1999 (MHSWR);
- Workplace (Health, Safety and Welfare) Regulations 1992 (WHSWR);
- Control of Substances Hazardous to Health Regulations 1994 (COSHH);
- Manual Handling Operations Regulations 1992 (MHOR).

It is also essential that the training is in line with:

- Sex Discrimination Acts of 1975 and 1986;
- Employment Protection (Consolidation) Act 1978;
- Employment Act 1980 and Social Security Act 1986;
- Equal Pay Act 1970, amended in 1983;
- Race Relations Act 1976;
- Discrimination Disability Act 1995.

In order to do this you must ensure that the materials and messages given do not discriminate against any trainee on the grounds of sex, marital status, race or disability. For example, does the timing of the course make it difficult for people with young children to attend?

9 Deciding on review and evaluation processes

At the end of the training you will want to measure what the programme has achieved. Now is the time to think about how you will do that.

There are a number of different methods you can use, some of which are listed below.

- **Evaluation questionnaires**

  Questionnaires that ask trainees to rate the training programme under a number of categories can be issued at the end of training.

- **Individual interviews with trainees**

  Individual interviews with trainees can be run at the end of the training. The interviewer will ask similar questions to the evaluation questionnaire but can probe in certain areas for more information.

- **Group discussion with trainees**

  Group discussions allow the trainer to get feedback from all the trainees at one time. It is quite economical with time but may not highlight problems encountered by individual trainees, as they may be reluctant to discuss these issues in front of the rest of the group.

- **Mid or end of programme tests**

  This is a way of testing the retention of underpinning knowledge. Tests can take the form of assignments, multiple choice questions, case studies or exam type questions. Trainees will need to be given some feedback on the results.

- **Work-based projects**

  At the end of a training programme trainees can be given a project to carry out at work that enables them to use the new skills and knowledge they have gained during the training. It is then possible to see the level of competence they have gained during training by the results of the project. It is important to make sure that the project is relevant to the training.

- **Observation of trainees at work**

  It is possible to observe the trainee, either formally or informally, once the training has been completed. You can then judge if new skills and knowledge are in evidence and being used at work.

Activity 37

5 mins

Which evaluation technique(s) will you use for your induction programme? Write the details in the space below.

_____

_____

_____

The types of evaluation technique you decide to use will obviously depend on the content of your programme, but hopefully you have selected one or more of the techniques we have discussed in this section.

10 Drawing up the training plan

You must record your training plan.

The planning part of your course is now complete; all you need to do is to record it.

There is no set way of recording your training plan but you may find the form on the next page a useful way of listing all the details.

Activity 38

15 mins

S/NVQ C9.3

This Activity may provide the basis of appropriate evidence for your S/NVQ portfolio. If you are intending to take this course of action, it might be better to write your answers on separate sheets of paper. You may need to use continuation sheets to complete your plan.

Using all the information you have put together during this workbook, use the Training Plan provided to write a training plan for an induction programme for new members of your team.

Training plan			
Course title:			
Intended audience:			
Date:		Time:	
Trainer:		Location:	
Objectives: By the end of the course the trainees will be able to:			
Assessment methods:			
Method of evaluation:			
Timing	Content	Method	Visual aids

Self-assessment 3

15 mins

1 In the workbook you were informed that training objectives should conform to the SMART principle. What does SMART stand for?

_____

_____

_____

2 What are the **four** stages of the learning cycle?

_____

_____

_____

_____

3 Fill in the gaps in the following sentences with appropriate words taken from the list below.

Coaching is a process of developing a _____ trained individual's

_____ and abilities through:

a issuing specific _____ tasks, which are _____ on completion;

b continuously _____ and _____ progress;

c holding _____ counselling sessions.

| APPRAISING | EXPERIENCE | PARTIALLY | REGULAR |
| ASSESSED | MONITORING | PLANNED | |

4 Complete the following sentences with suitable words.

a The objectives of training should be defined in terms of the desired improved work _____ of trainees.

b Training methods will need to be chosen bearing in mind:

■ the _____ of the trainees;

■ the demands of the_____;

■ the _____ of the budget;

■ the _____ available.

c Planning training effectively means getting the _____ right.

5 List some of the possible evaluation techniques you can build into your training plan.

_____

_____

_____

Answers to these questions can be found on pages 94–5.

11 Summary

- The ultimate purpose of all work-related training is to **improve work effectiveness**.

- Objectives should describe both **performance** and **standards**.

- Objectives should be **SMART**:

  S pecific
  M easurable
  A chievable
  R elevant
  T ime bound

- People **learn better** when they:

  - can **relate** what they are learning to something they already know and understand;
  - are **interested** in the topic being taught;
  - **take part actively** in the learning process, rather than simply listening or watching passively;
  - **discover information for themselves**, rather than being presented with it;
  - **respond actively** to what is being learned and are given **frequent and prompt reinforcement** to their responses;
  - are told the **governing principles** behind what they are learning;
  - are given **frequent summaries**;
  - are allowed to **learn at their own pace**;
  - are **motivated** to learn;
  - are allowed to learn in their **preferred learning style**.

- Both **on-the-job** and **off-the-job** training have advantages and disadvantages.

- Training **methods** available include:

  - demonstrations;
  - coaching;
  - talks and discussions;
  - films and videos;
  - mentoring;
  - open learning;
  - computer-based training;
  - interactive video.

Performance
checks

1 Quick quiz

Jot down the answers to the following questions on planning training.

Question 1   What is the main purpose of work training?

_____

_____

Question 2   List **three** benefits of training to the organization.

_____

_____

_____

Question 3   Training consists of passing on skills and knowledge. It also often involves
change. What types of change does it involve?

_____

_____

Question 4   List **two** benefits of training to the individual.

_____

_____

Question 5   What is meant by the performance gap?

_____

_____

_____

Question 6   Two of the stages of the training cycle are: Identify the training needs and Implement the plans. Name the other **two**.

_____

_____

Question 7   What is a versatility chart and what will it tell you?

_____

_____

_____

Question 8   Once you know which person has been trained in what tasks, can you be confident that you have identified your workteam's training needs? Give a brief reason for your answer.

_____

_____

_____

Question 9   Which organizational documents are most useful when it comes to defining training needs?

_____

_____

Question 10   What terms should the objectives of training be defined in?

_____

_____

_____

Question 11   As well as performance, what else should objectives describe?

_____

_____

Question 12   In what circumstances do people learn better? Can you give **two** points of learning theory?

_____

_____

_____

Question 13   State **two** advantages of training off the job.

_____

_____

Question 14   When managers are deciding on the best method of training, they must weigh up a number of considerations. Name **two** of these considerations.

_____

_____

Question 15   Describe **two** considerations which may affect the timing of training.

_____

_____

Answers to these questions can be found on pages 96–7.

2 Workbook assessment

60 mins

Read the following case and then deal with the questions which follow, writing your answers on a separate sheet of paper.

Derek Maloney had recently been placed in charge of a shift of operatives who worked in the shipping department of a food-processing organization. There were seven people in the workteam altogether. The factory produced a number of different food lines, some of which were perishable. Derek was responsible for:

■ keeping account of all the movements on a computerized stock control system;
■ directing traffic into and out of the loading bay areas;
■ moving the stock and loading the vehicles;
■ ensuring that the perishable lines did not exceed a defined time limit before being shipped.

Because of these difficult tasks, a multi-skilled workteam was needed. Some of Derek's workteam had been with the firm for a number of years, while others were fairly new. Among the skills and knowledge needed in the workteam were:

- computer keyboard skills;
- traffic direction;
- stock control clerical work, including processing the paperwork for the truck drivers;
- reading bar-coded tags and 'freshness indicators' with a hand-held terminal, and entering the data from this terminal into the computer system;
- loading vehicles in the correct way;
- safety control.

Two of the workteam were trained and experienced fork-lift truck drivers but all the workteam needed to be able to tackle any of the other tasks.

One of the problems facing Derek was training his workteam. This was complicated by the fact that the computer control system was about to be replaced. Derek was told by his boss that it was up to him to define the training needs for this workteam for the coming year.

You only need to write **one** or **two** sentences against each question.

1 What are likely to have been Derek's main training problems?

2 What are the first steps Derek should have taken in identifying the workteam's training needs?

3 What organizational documents might be useful to him?

4 Can you suggest some of the possible methods of training needs identification that he might use?

3 Work-based assignment

60 mins

S/NVQ C9.1, C9.3

The time guide for this assignment gives you an approximate idea of how long it is likely to take you to write up your findings. You will need to spend some additional time gathering information, perhaps talking to colleagues and thinking about the assignment. The results of your efforts should be presented on separate sheets of paper.

Your written response to this assignment may provide the basis of appropriate evidence for your S/NVQ portfolio.

For the purpose of this assignment, assume you are an off-the-job trainer.

1   Try to define your workteam's training needs for a specific period in the future – say the next six months – by answering the following questions.

- What are the objectives of your workteam for this period?
- In order to meet these objectives, what skills and/or knowledge will be required that are not readily available to you?
- Which members of the workteam need extra training?
- How will you go about planning the training your workteam needs over this period?

2   Construct a training plan similar to that in Activity 38.

3   In addition to this, explain and give some details on how you went about:

- analysing the training needs;
- planning the training;
- communicating with your workteam and others in your organization;
- using the training needs analysis and training plan to build your team;
- showing sensitivity when and where needed.

Reflect and review

1 Reflect and review

Now that you have completed your work on *Planning Training and Development*, let's review the workbook objectives.

You should be better able to:

■ describe the importance and benefits of training to you, your workteam and the organization you work for.

Everyone needs training. As the workbook has shown you, individuals need to be trained to carry out their jobs thoroughly, managers need training to make groups and workteams effective, and the whole organization needs training to produce the kind of skills and expertise required to meet the demands of its business.

You may want to ask yourself the following questions regarding this comment.

■ To what extent is training my workteam part of my role?

_____

_____

■ How involved should I get in highlighting the benefits of training to individuals, my workteam and my organization?

_____

_____

■ use different techniques to collect and analyse information for training needs analysis purposes.

Within the workbook we have introduced you to a number of techniques that can be used to collect and analyse the type of information you require for this purpose. We introduced you to job analysis techniques using job descriptions, talking to people and observing them. We looked at task analysis, which requires a more detailed study of the knowledge and skill demands of a task. We also studied the use of versatility charts, diff-rating scales and appraisal interviews. This range of techniques will give you a sufficiently broad sample to select from.

You may now need to consider the following.

■ Which of the techniques that you have been introduced to are suitable for use with your workteam?

_____

_____

■ Do you possess the necessary skills to carry out these techniques?

_____

_____

■ contribute to the identification of training and development needs for individuals and workteams.

If you have read this workbook carefully you will be aware that workteam training needs are derived from workteam objectives – which in turn must originate from the business strategy of the organization. You will also be aware that the manager must consider each member of the workteam individually and decide what each member needs to enable him or her to perform better. It is important that the manager play a role in this task.

Some questions to ask yourself here are these.

■ Do you consider this task to be part of your role?

_____

_____

■ How can the identification of training needs be fitted into the work schedule?

_____

_____

■ Should the appraisal interview have a part to play in the process?

_____

_____

- set objectives for training and development.

  Setting objectives is the first task when planning training as the trainer/manager must decide exactly what they are trying to achieve. Training objectives that are Specific, Measurable, Achievable, Relevant and Time bound will do this. In this workbook we asked you to write some training objectives for an induction programme.

  An issue for you to think about here is:

  - How can you ensure that all training programmes have objectives?

    _____

    _____

- contribute to planning training and development.

  When training needs are identified someone has to decide the details of how the training needs are to be met. The manager is in a unique position to make a significant contribution to this task. Managers know the workteams or the individuals well, and know what training methods would be most suitable and over what period of time the training should take place. They are also in a position to make recommendations on other issues, such as topics, on-the-job or off-the-job training, types of trainer etc. In this workbook we have introduced you to the issues around the subject of planning training and development.

  Some things for you to reflect on about this topic are:

  - What role do you think you should play in planning training and development?

    _____

    _____

  - What facilities, equipment and trainers are available to you for training?

    _____

    _____

  - Is there a budget for training?

    _____

    _____

  - What types of training methods do you think would be most suitable for your workteam?

    _____

    _____

■ draw up a training plan.

In the workbook we explained that once all the planning is done the decisions made need to be recorded. We also suggested how to record the training plan.

Final subjects you could think about are:

■ In what format do you want to record your training plans? Should this format be one the whole organization uses or just your department?

_____

_____

■ What part do you think you should play in drawing up a training plan?

_____

_____

2 Action plan

Use this plan to further develop for yourself a course of action you want to take. Make a note in the left-hand column of the issues or problems you want to tackle, and then decide what you intend to do, and make a note in column 2.

The resources you need might include time, materials, information or money. You may need to negotiate for some of them, but they could be something easily acquired, like half an hour of somebody's time, or a chapter of a book. Put whatever you need in column 3. No plan means anything without a timescale, so put a realistic target completion date in column 4.

Finally, describe the outcome you want to achieve as a result of this plan, whether it is for your own benefit or advancement, or a more efficient way of doing things.

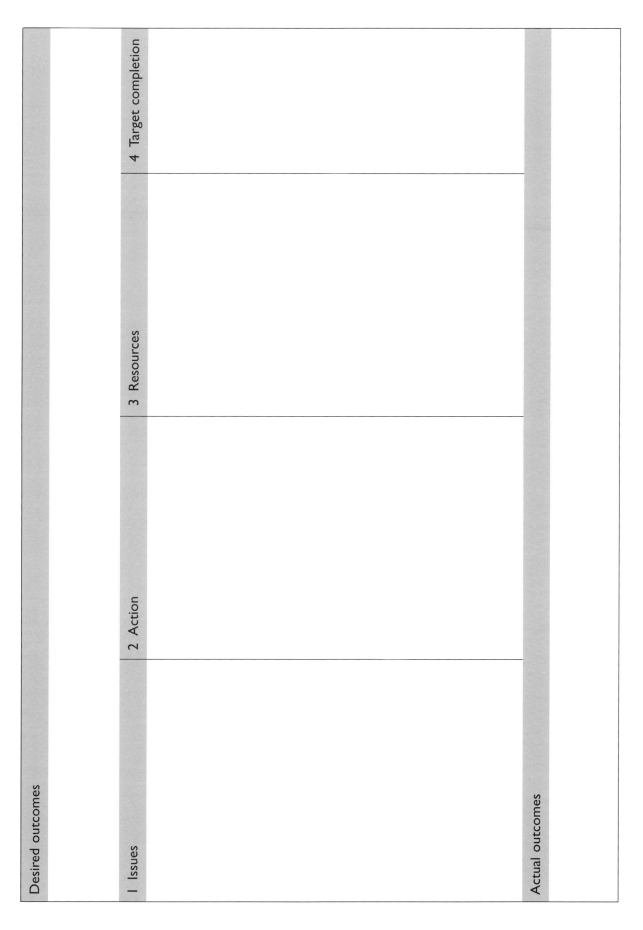

Desired outcomes

1 Issues

2 Action

3 Resources

4 Target completion

Actual outcomes

3 Extensions

Extension 1	Book	*Training Needs Analysis in the Workplace*
	Author	Robyn Peterson
	Edition	1998 (2nd edition)
	Publisher	Kogan Page
Extension 2	Open Learning	*The Trainer Development Programme: a flexible ten-day programme of workshop sessions*
	Author	Leslie Rae
	Edition	1994
	Publisher	Kogan Page
Extension 3	Book	*Creating a Training and Development Strategy*
	Author	Andrew Mayo
	Edition	1998
	Publisher	Chartered Institute of Personnel and Development
Extension 4	Book	*How to Write and Prepare Training Materials*
	Author	Nancy Stimson
	Edition	2002 (2nd edition)
	Publisher	Kogan Page

These extensions can be taken up via your ILM Centre. They will either have them or they will arrange access to them. However, it may be more convenient to check out the materials with your personnel or training people at work – they may well give you access. There are other good reasons for approaching your own people; for example they will become aware of your interest and you can involve them in your development.

4 Answers to self-assessment questions

Self-assessment 1 on page 23

1 a Training provides a means of getting SKILLS and KNOWLEDGE.

   b Training is a PLANNED procedure designed to improve the EFFECTIVE-NESS of people at work.

   c For training to be successful trainees may need to be convinced that the training is RELEVANT and IMPORTANT to them.

   d Training opens DOORS.

2 You may have listed any of the following.

From the organization's point of view, training:

- reduces learning time, so bringing new recruits to full working capacity more quickly;
- provides a means of getting jobs done more safely, efficiently and effectively;
- results in a workforce which is more flexible and better able to cope with change.

From the individual's point of view, training leads to:

- increased job satisfaction;
- improved self esteem;
- the possibility of promotion.

From the manager's point of view, training means:

- getting work done more safely, efficiently and effectively;
- improved workteam morale;
- greater flexibility, enabling change to be managed more easily.

More examples of the benefits of training were provided for you in Session A, section 4.

3 The missing words are:

Identify the TRAINING needs

Make PLANS and PREPARATIONS

IMPLEMENT the plans

Evaluate and FEED BACK the results

Reflect and review

Self-assessment 2 on page 53

Self-assessment 3 on page 79

1 SMART stands for Specific, Measurable, Achievable, Relevant and Time bound.

2 The four stages of the learning cycle are:

Stage 1 – Experience a learning activity;
Stage 2 – Review the learning experience;
Stage 3 – Draw conclusions from the learning experience;
Stage 4 – Plan the next steps.

3 Coaching is a process of developing a PARTIALLY trained individual's EXPERIENCE and abilities through:

a issuing specific, PLANNED tasks, which are ASSESSED on completion;
b continuously MONITORING and APPRAISING progress;
c holding REGULAR counselling sessions.

4 a The objectives of training should be defined in terms of the desired improved work PERFORMANCE of trainees.
b Training methods will need to be chosen bearing in mind:
   ■ the NEEDS of the trainees;
   ■ the demands of the TASK;

■ the CONSTRAINTS of the budget;
■ the RESOURCES available.

c Planning well means getting the DETAIL right.

5 Some of the evaluation techniques that you could build into your training plan are:

■ evaluation questionnaires;
■ individual interviews with trainees;
■ group discussion with trainees;
■ mid or end of programme tests;
■ work-based projects;
■ observation of trainees at work.

5 Answers to activities

**Activity 22
on page 43**

Task	d
Wages	0 (−3)
Purchase ledger	1
Sales ledger	0
Stock control	0
Work allocation	1
Control and checking	1
Customer complaints	0
Payment authorization	1
Customer enquiries	1
Data input	0
General admin	0
Word processing	2

Column (d) shows the number of people who require training. The areas for training are as follows.

Purchase ledger	1 person
Work allocation	1 person
Control and checking	1 person
Payment authorization	1 person
Customer enquiries	1 person
Word processing	2 people

6 Answers to the quick quiz

Answer 1   The main purpose of work training is to improve the effectiveness of people at work.

Answer 2   The benefits of training to the organization include:

- reducing learning time;
- getting jobs done more safely, efficiently and effectively;
- having a more flexible and efficient work force, that is better able to cope with change;
- improvement in morale and motivation of employees;
- reducing the number of customer complaints;
- reducing the number of problems with suppliers;
- increased profitability through increased output or reduced costs.

Answer 3   Training often involves changing attitudes.

Answer 4   The benefits of training to the individual include:

- increased job satisfaction;
- improved self-esteem;
- a greater potential for promotion;
- increased opportunities.

Answer 5   The performance gap is the difference between the way things are and the way you'd like things to be. For example between:

- how well the workteam is performing and how well you'd like it to perform;
- what workteam members know and understand and what they ought to know and understand.

Answer 6   The other two stages of the training cycle are:

- make plans and preparations;
- evaluate and feed back the results.

Answer 7   A versatility chart contains a list of team members and the jobs of the department. It is used to show who is competent to do which jobs.

Answer 8   The answer to this question should be no. The reason for this is that versatility charts don't tell you what the training needs are beyond the normal functions of the workteam. They don't allow for the fact that some jobs consist of skills that can be learned quickly by any workteam member. Nor do they allow for the range of skills and knowledge some other jobs may require. They also do not give any indication of the degree of expertise reached by the person currently holding the job.

Answer 9   When defining training needs the most useful organizational documents are job descriptions and person specifications.

Answer 10   The objectives of training are defined in terms of the desired work performance of the trainees.

Answer 11   Objectives should describe both performance and standards.

Answer 12   People learn more easily when they:

- can relate the subject matter to something they already know and understand;
- are interested in the subject matter;
- take an active part in the learning process, rather than simply listening and watching passively;
- discover information for themselves rather than being presented with it.

Answer 13   Advantages of training off-the-job are:

- a better chance to concentrate away from distractions of the workplace, such as noise and bustle;
- freedom from interruptions and from having to put effort into work;
- an opportunity to think through the principles behind actions and perhaps to question why the work is done in the way it is.

Answer 14   Managers need to consider the following:

- the needs of the trainees;
- the demands of the task;
- the constraints of the budget and available resources.

Answer 15   The following may affect the timing of training:

- the need for the trainee's absence at work to be covered;
- that all the trainees and the facilities are available at the time you need them;
- when the new knowledge or skills will need to be applied.

7 Certificate

Completion of this certificate by an authorized person shows that you have worked through all the parts of this workbook and satisfactorily completed the assessments. The certificate provides a record of what you have done that may be used for exemptions or as evidence of prior learning against other nationally certificated qualifications.

Pergamon Flexible Learning and ILM are always keen to refine and improve their products. One of the key sources of information to help this process are people who have just used the product. If you have any information or views, good or bad, please pass these on.

INSTITUTE OF LEADERSHIP & MANAGEMENT

SUPERSERIES

Planning
Training and Development

....

has satisfactorily completed this workbook

Name of signatory   ....

Position   ....

Signature   ....

Date   ....

Official stamp

Fourth Edition

INSTITUTE OF LEADERSHIP & MANAGEMENT
SUPERSERIES
FOURTH EDITION

Achieving Quality	0 7506 5874 6
Appraising Performance	0 7506 5838 X
Becoming More Effective	0 7506 5887 8
Budgeting for Better Performance	0 7506 5880 0
Caring for the Customer	0 7506 5840 1
Collecting Information	0 7506 5888 6
Commitment to Equality	0 7506 5893 2
Controlling Costs	0 7506 5842 8
Controlling Physical Resources	0 7506 5886 X
Delegating Effectively	0 7506 5816 9
Delivering Training	0 7506 5870 3
Effective Meetings at Work	0 7506 5882 7
Improving Efficiency	0 7506 5871 1
Information in Management	0 7506 5890 8
Leading Your Team	0 7506 5839 8
Making a Financial Case	0 7506 5892 4
Making Communication Work	0 7506 5875 4
Managing Change	0 7506 5879 7
Managing Lawfully – Health, Safety and Environment	0 7506 5841 X
Managing Lawfully – People and Employment	0 7506 5853 3
Managing Relationships at Work	0 7506 5891 6
Managing Time	0 7506 5877 0
Managing Tough Times	0 7506 5817 7
Marketing and Selling	0 7506 5837 1
Motivating People	0 7506 5836 3
Networking and Sharing Information	0 7506 5885 1
Organizational Culture and Context	0 7506 5884 3
Organizational Environment	0 7506 5889 4
Planning and Controlling Work	0 7506 5813 4
Planning Training and Development	0 7506 5860 6
Preventing Accidents	0 7506 5835 5
Project and Report Writing	0 7506 5876 2
Securing the Right People	0 7506 5822 3
Solving Problems	0 7506 5818 5
Storing and Retrieving Information	0 7506 5894 0
Understanding Change	0 7506 5878 9
Understanding Finance	0 7506 5815 0
Understanding Quality	0 7506 5881 9
Working In Teams	0 7506 5814 2
Writing Effectively	0 7506 5883 5

To order – phone us direct for prices and availability details
(please quote ISBNs when ordering) on 01865 888190